WORKING IN THE

Smart!Zone™

Smart Strategies to Be a Top Performer at Work and at Home

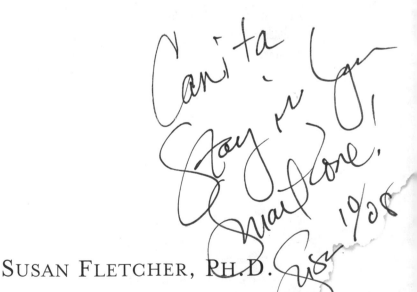

Canita
Stay in your
Smart!Zone,
Susan 1/08

SUSAN FLETCHER, PH.D.

For more information contact:
Susan Fletcher, Ph.D.
Smart Zone Solutions
2301 Ohio Drive, Suite 135
Plano, Texas 75093
972 612-1188
www.SmartZoneExpert.com
www.FletcherPhD.com

Printed in the United States of America on acid-free paper
12 11 10 09 08   10 9 8 7 6 5 4 3 2 1

First Edition

Table of Contents

Foreword

Psychologist Dr. Susan Fletcher asks her patients and clients, "What can we do to make this situation better?" and "How can you contribute to the solution?" Susan can help people find and close the emotional intelligence gap and increase a person's success.

For some people there may be a trust issue; for others there may be an inability to manage perception; for another, it could be difficulty handling change. Susan has built a model for how to live a more efficient and more productive life in the Smart Zone.

It is my belief that the absence of clarity drains organizational energy and that lack of focus produces a culture of indecisiveness. This results in the inability of business leaders to execute their vision of success.

Susan's Smart Zone strategies are the basis for high performing relationships and are a key component to providing clarity and focus. Smart Zone strategies, with the foundational components of emotional intelligence and trust, outline essential attributes required of today's leading CEO's and executives.

I first met Susan in 2000 and in July 2004 she visited my Success Acceleration Studio where I meet regularly with many of the world's top CEO's. We discussed the basis of her Smart Zone model and how it had helped patients in her clinical practice. She was already the opening speaker for national conferences and meetings making the cross over to working with key leaders in corporations.

It was then that I knew Susan had clarity about keeping people in the Smart Zone, she was clearly focused on the development of her model, and now with *Working in the Smart Zone*, she has executed her mission to bring her Smart Zone strategies to you.

In her book, *Working in the Smart Zone*, Susan provides an explanation and execution strategy for releasing the worry and stress that can hold back your performance both at work and at home. She provides concrete ways along with real life examples of how to stay productive even in the face of organizational change. In addition, she provides a way to look inward to better handle your own emotions and improve relationships with friends, family and co-workers.

In my business I use the term Return on Effort (ROE) to describe when significant reductions in time can be achieved relative to the actual results produced. *Working in the Smart Zone* is definitely worth your time which is why I recommend it to anyone looking to go to the next level.

Tony Jeary, 2008
Coach to the World's Top CEOs

Acknowledgments

Working on this book was a different experience than our first book, *Parenting in the Smart Zone*. This book required us to bring what I do on the platform as a speaker and in board rooms as a consultant into easily digestible written form. That proved to be more difficult than we expected but no less rewarding. We are proud of what we have accomplished with this book and I have had a support team that has made sure that we practiced what we preached creating a book we could all be proud to present to you.

Zan Jones is the wizard behind the curtain. She "gets" me and has helped me get me. As our Director of Client Relations she books our speaking and makes sure I have what I need to hit the mark as a speaker and consultant. With this project, she served as my chief straight shooter. She kept my spirits up, listened when I needed to vent, and provided many snippets to keep our content on the mark. She knows what to say to me and how to help us say it to you.

Sharon Beck is the best funky chicken who has kept things rolling in the clinical practice as I gave attention to this project and did all the travel. This has been a difficult year and Sharon has grown more than the rest of us. Her loyalty has been cherished and her diverse skills have been needed. While she has threatened to change her ring tone when I call to something less than desirable, I know she will always answer and her involvement has been much appreciated.

Brenda Quinn came along towards the end to edit. My experience in the past with editors has been grueling. My experience with Brenda has been quite the opposite. When I saw what an impact she made on the manuscript, I found the experience to be great. Thanks Brenda for not sounding like an eighth grade English teacher. I learned to welcome your edits and we were obviously better for it.

Clint Greenleaf and his crowd came through again. From a beach in Florida, you made it happen. Thank you for your response. You are what you promise.

Tony Jeary—thanks for being there and for helping me own the word "Smart."

To my Vistage group and Nancy Starr. I'm glad to be a part of a group of such talented CEOs. Your ability to hold me accountable in my clinical practice and in Smart Zone Solutions helped free my attention and energy to complete this project. You helped me focus and shortened my learning curve.

To my cherished girlfriends Julie Nash, Kathi Stacy, Camille Joiner, Marjie Sands, and Cathy Evans: I have needed the times we have been together and look forward to now having more. Thanks for making me important to you,

Finally I thank my family—especially my husband Mark. For this book I was absent more and up at night later. There have been a lot of unfinished projects like those chairs in the garage I want to redo. I've needed you to overlook some things and that can't be easy.

To Alex, Chase, and Sam: Thanks for not growing up too fast. I wouldn't want to miss it. You all mean the world to me. You are my first and most important job and everything else comes second. You are the energy in my Smart Zone.

Introduction

The Day I Stole
Mr. McAfee's Underwear

It's just before Christmas. In two days we're supposed to leave for the holidays, and there are still so many things to do at work and for home. I stayed up late last night and finished the Christmas cards, did a bunch of paperwork for work, and got through the piles of laundry. Today I feel rushed, tired and a bit overwhelmed, which is understandable. I know that I'm out of my Smart Zone™*. I keep thinking, if I can sleep in during the holidays I'll get caught up.

But tonight I still have one more errand before I can collapse into bed. Alex, our 11-year-old, came home from school today with his shoes so beaten up that he can't wear them any longer. Weren't those shoes fine this morning? Didn't we buy those shoes just the other day?

We head to Academy, a sporting goods store by our house, to look at shoes. There is no way I'm going to Super Target or the mall for shoes tonight since I want to avoid the crowds of people who are still shopping for the holidays. It's just easier to get some shoes at Academy. Anything to make life easier.

As we're finishing at the checkout line, I see Carie McAfee is behind us. I can't remember the last time I saw Carie, but I'm happy to run into her. Just last week my husband and I saw her husband, Jim, when we were picking up our 5th graders from their week at camp, and Jim told us about the camp their son Ryan would be going to the following summer. My husband and I had already decided that Alex would enjoy that camp, so we were excited to hear that Ryan McAfee will be at the same camp.

So of course when I see Carie at Academy, we talk about camp as she pays for her items. I'm so tired that I don't even think I'm smiling but inside my head I'm taking notes. I need to register Alex for the same week at camp as Ryan. I need to remember what week she tells me Ryan is going.

I'm aware that my brain can handle only a few thoughts at a time. I feel like a computer that's close to capacity—there's so little free disk space left. I wonder how full the disk can get before the system will shut down. It's overwhelming to have so many different things happening all day long, for so many days in a row, at work and at home. So I grab our package and head home. When I walk in the door I reach into the bag. But I don't find Alex's shoes. I find men's underwear. Jim McAfee's underwear.

Believe it or not, it takes me a while to figure out why I have a bag of men's clothing. Alex begins to laugh. It turns out he had picked up

*Smart Zone™ is a registered trademark of Smart Zone Solutions.

the bag with his shoes while Carie and I were talking. He thinks it's funny that I've come home with Mr. McAfee's underwear. No. The truth is I STOLE Mr. McAfee's underwear.

This is what it looks like to be out of your Smart Zone.

Has this ever happened to you?

What is the Smart Zone?

The Smart Zone is a mental state for optimal performance using intellect, emotions, and behaviors. Everyone can develop their own best practices to enhance focus, balance, and perspective to successfully meet the challenges at home and at work.

The Smart Zone strategies in this book have been developed from our experience in more than 20 years of clinical practice and consulting. We have worked with a wide variety of companies, including The Staubach Company, BNSF Railway, Raytheon, Southwest Airlines, credit unions in Texas, Florida, California, New Jersey and New Mexico, Rosenbauer Firefighting Technology, Federal Reserve Bank, and EmCare. These and many other organizations have come to us because they want to solicit the best from each employee and build the most successful organization possible.

When we're working with key leaders in companies, both large and small, we often hear people talk about making mistakes they wouldn't normally make. They describe feeling disconnected and otherwise occupied, making careless errors, and working less effectively. This led us to identify that everyone has what I call a Smart Zone, where they are able to work to the best of their ability.

In our consulting work, we help people stay in their Smart Zone so they can increase their productivity, increase their efficiency, and ultimately get more satisfaction on a day-to-day basis. Organizations using Smart Zone strategies are more productive. And because an increase in productivity adds to the bottom line, organizations using Smart Zone strategies are also more profitable.

The Smart Zone is where you work to the best of your ability, *emotionally*, *intellectually*, and *behaviorally*. If you shudder at the idea of getting in touch with your softer side, let me tell you why being in the Smart Zone is critical. It's a tough, competitive business world out there, and it's absolutely imperative that businesses retain top talent, get lean and be more competitive, increase efficiency and produce stellar products and services. Being in the Smart Zone helps the bottom line because Smart Zone thinking keeps people in the mindset of working to the best of their ability.

Are you being asked to do more with less? When you're out of your Smart Zone you're more likely to make mistakes that cost time and money.

We're going to talk about 10 individual strategies that you can use to get in your Smart Zone and stay in your Smart Zone. These strategies can be incorporated into everything you do. The beauty of the Smart Zone strategies is that they apply at the office and also at home, no matter what your lifestyle.

Because you're reading this book, we know you're already looking for ways to increase your productivity and the productivity of your organization. Learning these things for yourself is an important first step, but it's just as important to extend the Smart Zone way of doing things to those you do business with, those you live with, and those you want to be with as you manage your life.

How to Use This Book

This book has three parts. Each one will help you maximize your ability to build a Smart Zone community around you.

Part One describes the Smart Zone model, its two key concepts—Emotional Intelligence and Trust—and the 10 strategies. Learn the model and use it to keep yourself and your organization in the Smart Zone! Each chapter ends with *Smart Moves*, which summarize key concepts from the chapter.

Part Two presents *The Smart Zone Life Plan*, a set of strategies and worksheets that will give you the tools to develop the *6 Competencies for a Business Person* and the *8 Competencies for a Smart Zone Lifestyle*. Part Two also lists invaluable resources that will help you stay in the Smart Zone to continue to be the best you can be by learning and growing personally and professionally.

Part Three gives you *The Ultimate Smart Moves*. These include some of the Smart Moves from Part One that provide such high value that they deserve their own chapters. Ultimate Smart Moves can be used again and again to keep you on track… *Working in the Smart Zone*.

PART ONE

Working in the Smart Zone

Chapter 1

*The Smart Zone Model
and How It Can Work for You*

The Smart Zone Model

In The Smart!Zone™

More Productive
More Efficient

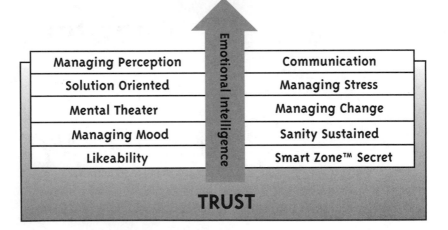

Managing Perception		Communication
Solution Oriented		Managing Stress
Mental Theater	Emotional Intelligence	Managing Change
Managing Mood		Sanity Sustained
Likeability		Smart Zone™ Secret

TRUST

The Smart Zone Model begins with two foundational key concepts—**Emotional Intelligence (EQ)** and **Trust**. There is a lot of evidence to prove that high-performing organizations are more Emotionally Intelligent and have High Trust cultures. In the chapters that follow, we will show you this evidence.

The model builds on these two concepts with 10 strategies that will help your organization grow and sustain its gains from *Working in the Smart Zone*. These 10 strategies are based on performance-enhancing business practices that will tune and calibrate your performance.

Every organization must have a results-driven culture. An organization that embraces the concept of *Working in the Smart Zone* wants to be highly effective and produce results. Many organizations have discovered the value of raising an organization's EQ and creating a High Trust environment, and are incorporating those concepts into their leadership training. But only the Smart Zone Model provides 10 strategies that will help you create a climate of Smart Zone thinking.

The Value of Self-Management Skills

Most people will say that they earned the best grades in college when they took a full load of classes and also held down a job. It doesn't really make sense that more work (having a job *and* going to college) created better outcomes (higher grades). Wouldn't you just burn out from so much responsibility so young? Actually, no. When people know they have limited time to complete a task, they rise to the occasion and manage themselves. Okay, not everyone will. But those in the Smart Zone will!

Workers with high work pressures and poor self-management skills miss work twice as often as workers with strong self-management skills. Self-management skills help you cope better with work pressures because they help you:

- organize yourself
- anticipate conflicts
- manage your impulses
- minimize distractions
- keep yourself alert

If you read this list again you'll probably think of people who count on *others* to do all those things *for* them. Those people have poor self-management skills. Organizations value people with good self-management skills because they're the most productive, need less supervision, and are self starters.

Time Management is for Rookies

While you're learning to Work in the Smart Zone, let's get one thing straight from the beginning. Time management is for rookies. Working in the Smart Zone is about managing your **attention** and your **energy**—not just managing the hours in the day. People in the Smart Zone take inventory of those things in life that drain them, and they try to minimize or even eliminate them. Stack the deck in your favor by including things in your life that give you energy. You'll be glad you did.

Every company I consult with tells me that they are being asked to do more with less. Maybe you've considered buying a BlackBerry or other device to help keep yourself organized and manage your work and personal life. You may not realize that there is no magic tool you can buy that can keep you on task throughout the day. But you *can* stay in your Smart Zone and increase your productivity by managing your behavior, your emotions, and the way you think.

Self-management is about more than managing time. By following these Smart Ideas you can have a productive day *and* have time for yourself, and you'll avoid the mistake of thinking time management alone will increase your productivity.

- **Be selfish with your yes's**. Learn to prioritize, and manage your ability to use your yes's wisely. There are many tasks to complete but some are more negotiable. Be intentional about what you commit to. Does the commitment fit into your overall strategy and focus? Are you committed to this task or are you saying yes because someone else expects it? Choose two things you have a choice about and just say no.

- **Look at but don't answer email first thing in the morning**. Many people waste a lot of time and energy early in the morning getting lost in their email. But they don't realize that they're setting a negative pace for the day. Unless you're very disciplined and have mastered one- or two-sentence responses, you use a lot of time and energy gathering your thoughts for emails that can range from managing the budget for a project at work to who will drive for the next Boy Scout campout. Review emails in the morning but get in the habit of setting aside a dedicated block of time to respond. Stick to the schedule and you'll avoid getting lost in email adventures that misuse your energy and attention.

- **Master the ability to end conversations that are not productive**. If at the end of the day you wonder where the time went, learn to monitor your downtime at work. How many people dropped by to shoot the bull? When you have to call someone who could keep you on the phone too long, say up front, "I only have a minute but I wanted to get back to you before this afternoon." That sets the expectation that the call will be short.

- **Let the phone ring.** Growing up, I remember my parents taking the phone off the hook while we ate dinner. I didn't like it as a teenager, but now as a parent I see the value in uninterrupted family time. When you're in the middle of a task at work, whenever possible don't let the phone interrupt you. Finish your thought, finish the task, and then respond to the voicemail. Shifting constantly between tasks can interfere with your attention and drain your energy. Don't let someone else determine the pace of your day.

- **Make lists and notes in a central place you can always have with you**. When you write something down, you're more likely to do it. But make your list on something that you're likely to keep with you. Sticky notes and napkins get lost because they seem unimportant. Carry a small journal with blank pages—preferably the kind that also holds a pen—so you can easily write down things that you value, and then make sure you keep the journal with you. This way you are less likely to lose a good idea or the information you need to follow up with someone.

The Smart Zone Model outlines the ways you can be *Working in the Smart Zone*. The following chapters describe the two major concepts, Emotional Intelligence and Trust, and each of the 10 strategies in the

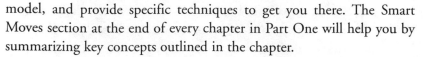

model, and provide specific techniques to get you there. The Smart Moves section at the end of every chapter in Part One will help you by summarizing key concepts outlined in the chapter.

Now that you know the Smart Zone Model, get ready to start *Working in the Smart Zone.*

SMART Moves

- The Smart Zone Model is based on Emotional Intelligence (EQ) and Trust. High performing organizations are more Emotionally Intelligent and have High Trust cultures.

- Self-management is about more than managing the hours in the day. Instead, managing your attention and your energy will help you stay in the Smart Zone.

- Increase your productivity by managing your behavior, your emotions, and the way you think. Prioritize your commitments, and be intentional about those you choose to take on. Make sure they fit with your overall strategy. Email can consume valuable hours. Schedule time to answer email so that you keep control of your day.

Chapter 2

Emotional Intelligence

"As much as 80% of adult success comes from EQ."
– Daniel Goleman

The History of Emotional Intelligence

In 1996 author Daniel Goleman introduced the term Emotional Intelligence (EQ), which he defined as a set of competencies that distinguish how people manage feelings, interact, and communicate.

Research shows that our ability to manage our emotions and relationships with others is twice as important as our intelligence quotient (IQ), and that organizations with higher Emotional Intelligence predicted success. A high EQ is essential for those in positions of leadership and for anyone who wants to increase the productivity and satisfaction in their life.

Even though the concept of EQ appears to be new in the workplace, in the times of Aristotle there was recognition that managing emotions was important.

"Anyone can become angry—that is easy. But to be
angry with the right person, to the right degree,
at the right time, for the right purpose,
and in the right way—that is not easy."
– Aristotle

Emotional Intelligence in the Workplace

In the workplace, EQ skills are the "people smart" skills that make some employees more valuable than others. To lead effectively, it's important that leaders be skilled at managing their own emotions and the emotions of others.

The ability to use emotions effectively is the foundation of high-performing relationships. Individual relationships create the workplace environment, and the climate shapes the way employees and customers relate.

Emotions provide the energy to execute our best thinking. The more emotional and social sense you have, the easier it is to go efficiently and productively about your life.

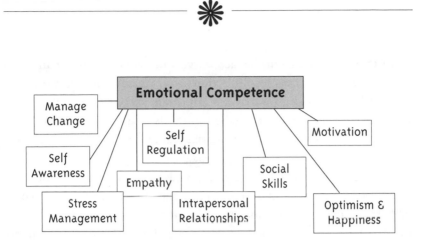

Although there are a few different models of EQ, most of them concentrate on the following:

- The relationship with and awareness of yourself
- The relationship you have with others
- Your ability to regulate your own emotions
- Your ability to manage stress and impulses
- Your level of optimism and happiness
- Your ability to be adaptable and manage change
- Your ability to be empathetic
- Your ability to self-motivate
- Your ability to be socially skilled

Everyone has the potential to develop a higher EQ by being deliberate about what it is, what it looks like, what strategies move it forward, and what it can produce. As with any fundamental shift in culture, time is needed to build an Emotionally Intelligent environment. There are no quick fixes in the development of EQ.

Do People With a High EQ Have to Wear Pink?

When I discuss EQ principles with key leaders in organizations, many of the men wrongly presume that being Emotionally Intelligent means being more feminine in your thinking and in your actions. That couldn't

be further from the truth. In fact, we've worked with more than a few women who could use a few EQ points to increase their career success.

For both men and women, it's important to build an environment where EQ is valued. In fact, the best example I have of a high-EQ environment, and one of my favorite stories, came from a speech to a mostly male audience of over 600 engineers.

The group we presented to had a wide diversity in age, education, length of employment, and initial acceptance to having a woman come talk about "emotional competency." From the interviews we did before the event we knew that key leaders were skeptical. No non-industry expert had ever before been invited to a quarterly meeting.

We were pretty prepared for the reaction we might get from the engineers who had been told by their CEO that a woman was coming to talk with them about their emotions. I'm the daughter of an engineer and I also married an engineer, so I knew from experience that my discussion of emotions would need to develop slowly. Not that engineers are not Emotionally Intelligent—it's just that they tend to think in spreadsheets. I was going to ask them to take their emotional competencies beyond their norm and develop action plans for growth. I didn't want to turn them off the idea of *Working in the Smart Zone*.

Even in an audience of 600 we strive for interaction and try to raise the energy of the group so the learning provides the most value. I'm sure more than a few thought I might make them embrace or say "affirmations" to each other. As I explained how EQ can help move an organization towards greater productivity and financial success, I mentioned that I was aware that there was one department that always met their quarterly numbers and seemed to have the lowest rate of safety incidents. The same department met both goals. Go figure!

As I continued to talk about how EQ increases productivity, I asked them to talk in small groups at their seats about what they were already doing that would be considered Emotionally Intelligent. I walked around the room and heard a number of good examples of how they create an environment where people want to work. But two stories in particular stood out, both from the department that always met its quarterly numbers and had the lowest rate of safety incidents.

George is a valued employee who had worked for

the company for over 15 years. His department of 18 people worked hard to manage the manufacturing of a specific system that was key to the development of their product. Two summers ago, George took four weeks of medical leave for eye surgery that also required him to wear a patch for at least four more weeks after returning to work. George was apprehensive about being out for such a long time and then returning with an eye patch. He knew his long leave would cause stress in the department.

During his four-week leave, almost all 17 of his co-workers kept in touch, assuring him that although they were making do without him they looked forward to his return.

George felt very valued during his medical leave and told his wife that he was eager to return to work, since he felt bored and not useful while at home. He was a bit apprehensive, though, about having to wear the eye patch while at work. He didn't dare mention it to his co-workers since he already felt sensitive enough about being out and coming back looking like a pirate.

Finally the Monday came around when he was scheduled to return to work. As George walked in the building, the guard welcomed him back, and most of the people walking the halls gave their typical "Good morning." George felt butterflies in his stomach as he walked to his department.

Entering the room, he saw his co-workers at their desks with their backs to him, seeming to not notice his return. As George put his lunch bag on his desk and quietly said, "Good morning," as if on cue all 17 of his co-workers turned towards him. They were wearing eye patches just like George so that he wouldn't feel so self-conscious about his appearance. George laughed from deep inside, in a way he hadn't done in a while. He thought it had been quite an effort for them to coordinate this stunt. But what he wasn't prepared for was that they were committed to wearing their patches for as long as George wore his.

In true EQ fashion this act of friendship solidified an emotional response that shows that people smarts build loyalty and inspire exceptional motivation and productivity.

From this same group came another example of how important it is to consider the importance of EQ in developing a workplace where people want to be.

Meeting quarterly numbers is a common goal among all the departments. But no matter how hard most departments tried, they came up short. Not George's department. They managed every quarter to embrace the challenge and meet their numbers. How did they do it?

It all came together at the local go-cart track.

In George's department, each person had a specific contribution to meet the quarterly goals. Since you can only manage what you can measure, George's department developed a chart of their quarterly goals that remained visible for everyone to see. Quarterly numbers ended on a Friday and were typically posted on a Monday. There was always eagerness to see the results.

Once the numbers were made public, the real motivation began. In this company there was healthy competition—a sense of belonging and a sense that everyone was a part of something bigger. There was also a sense of creativity that made it a place where they wanted to work and had jobs they wanted to do.

On the Friday after the numbers were revealed, people in the department gathered at the local go-cart track to race in the quarterly competition. Those who had met their individual goals were ranked and those with the greatest success were lined up a few feet ahead of their colleagues. Consider it like teeing off from the women's tees in golf. The race would begin and after a fierce competition a winner would be declared. But the best part was not about the race—it was all about the trophy.

They showed me the trophy. Although not the Heisman, it is still a coveted prize. The winner of the race is presented the trophy in a covered case, but the real prize was still to come. You see, the real prize is the opportunity to add something to the trophy, which is then displayed in the cube of the new winner. This builds a sense of camaraderie, adventure, collaboration, and excitement. Not until the big reveal do members of the group get to see the new addition.

Success is More About EQ Than IQ

UCLA research indicates that only 7% of leadership success is attributable to intellect, but a full 93% of success comes from trust, integrity, authenticity, honesty, creativity, presence, and resilience. It's not enough anymore to just be smart. You have to be people smart to succeed.

Consider these findings, which were prepared for the Consortium for Research on Emotional Intelligence in Organizations by Cary Cherniss, Ph.D., of Rutgers University.

- Of 515 senior executives analyzed by the search firm Egon Zehnder International, those who were primarily strong in emotional intelligence were more likely to succeed than those who were strongest in either relevant previous experience or IQ. In other words, Emotional Intelligence was a better predictor of success than either relevant previous experience or high IQ. More specifically, executives were high in Emotional Intelligence in 74% of the successes and only in 24% of the failures. The study included executives in Latin America, Germany, and Japan, and the results were almost identical in all three cultures.

- In a national insurance company, sales agents who were weak in emotional competencies such as self-confidence, initiative, and empathy sold policies with an average premium of $54,000. Those who were very strong in at least 5 of 8 key emotional

competencies sold policies worth $114,000 (Hay/McBer
Research and Innovation Group, 1997).

- In a large beverage firm that used standard hiring methods, 50%
of division presidents left within two years, mostly because of
poor performance. When the firm started hiring based on emotional competencies such as initiative, self-confidence, and leadership, only 6% left in two years. Furthermore, 87% of those
executives selected for their emotional competence were in the
top third of salary bonuses for performance in the divisions they
led. In addition, division leaders with these competencies outper-
formed their targets by 15 to 20%. Those who lacked them
underperformed by almost 20% (McClelland, 1999).

- Research by the Center for Creative Leadership has found that
the primary causes of career derailment in executives involve
deficits in emotional competence, particularly difficulty in handling change, not being able to work well in a team, and poor
interpersonal relations.

- At L'Oreal, sales agents selected on the basis of certain emotional
competencies significantly outsold salespeople selected using the
company's old selection procedure. On an annual basis, salespeople
selected on the basis of emotional competence sold $91,370 more
than did other salespeople, for a net revenue increase of $2.5 mil-
lion. Salespeople selected on the basis of emotional competence also
had 63% less turnover during the first year than did those selected
in the typical way (Spencer & Spencer, 1993; Spencer, McClelland,
& Kelner, 1997).

- An analysis of more than 300 top-level executives from 15 global
companies showed that six emotional competencies distinguished
the stars from the more average executives: influence, team leadership, organizational awareness, self-confidence, achievement drive,
and leadership (L.M. Spencer, Jr., 1997).

- After supervisors in a manufacturing plant received training in
emotional competencies, such as how to listen better and help
employees resolve problems on their own, lost-time accidents
were reduced by 50%, the average number of formal grievances

per year was reduced from 15 to 3, and the plant exceeded productivity goals by $250,000 (Pesuric & Byham, 1996). In another manufacturing plant where supervisors received similar training, production increased 17%. There was no such increase in production for a group of matched supervisors who were not trained (Porras & Anderson, 1981).

- One of the foundations of emotional competence, accurate self-assessment, was associated with superior performance among several hundred managers from 12 different organizations (Boyatzis, 1982).

- Another emotional competence, the ability to handle stress, was linked to success as a store manager in a retail chain. The most successful store managers were those best able to handle stress. Success was based on net profits, sales per square foot, sales per employee, and per-dollar inventory investment (Lusch & Serpkeuci, 1990).

- Optimism is another emotional competence that leads to increased productivity. New sales people at Met Life who scored high on a test of learned optimism sold 37% more life insurance in their first two years than did pessimists (Seligman, 1990).

- A study of 130 executives found that people's ability to handle their own emotions determined how much others preferred to deal with them (Walter V. Clarke Associates, 1997).

- Among sales reps at a computer company, those hired based on their emotional competence were 90% more likely to finish their training than were those hired on other criteria (Hay/McBer Research and Innovation Group, 1997).

- At a national furniture retailer, sales people hired based on emotional competence had half the dropout rate during their first year (Hay/McBer Research and Innovation Group, 1997).

- Financial advisors at American Express whose managers had completed the Emotional Competence training program were compared to an equal number whose managers had not. During the year following training, advisors working for trained managers grew their businesses by 18.1% compared to 16.2% for those whose managers were untrained.

- The most successful debt collectors in a large collection agency averaged 163% of goal attainment over a three-month period. They were compared with a group of collectors who achieved an average of only 80% over the same time period. The most successful collectors scored significantly higher in the emotional intelligence competencies of self-actualization, independence, and optimism. (Self-actualization refers to a well-developed inner knowledge of one's own goals and a sense of pride in one's work.) (Bachman et al., 2000).

How EQ Can Be Measured

Unlike IQ, EQ skills can be dramatically improved through awareness and training. We provide assessments in both our clinical practice and our consulting practice because the assessment provides so much value for EQ development. We use The BarOn Emotional Quotient Inventory (EQ-i) to assess EQ for individuals. Once we have individual assessments, we are able to present key leaders with a profile of the organization by group, department or team, and each participant can also compare his or her results with the group results. Individual results are kept confidential while group results are presented without identifying information.

Information about the EQ-i is available on our website: www.SmartZoneExpert.com. If you would like to schedule an EQ assessment for yourself, contact me at Susan@SmartZoneExpert.com.

Consider this:

> The U.S. Air Force used the EQ-i to select recruiters (the Air Force's frontline HR personnel) and found that the most successful recruiters scored significantly higher in the emotional intelligence competencies of Assertiveness, Empathy, Happiness, and Emotional Self-Awareness. The Air Force also found that by using Emotional Intelligence to select recruiters, they increased their ability to predict successful recruiters by nearly threefold. The immediate gain was a savings of $3 million annually. These gains resulted in the

Government Accounting Office submitting a report to Congress, which led to a request that the Secretary of Defense order all branches of the armed forces to adopt this procedure in recruitment and selection. (The GAO report, *Military Recruiting: The Department of Defense Could Improve Its Recruiter Selection and Incentive Systems,* was submitted to Congress January 30, 1998. Richard Handley and Reuven Bar-On provided this information.)

Roadblocks to EQ Development: Know Your Blind Spots

Robert E. Kaplan studied 42 highly successful executives and found that there was less self awareness if the executives had blind spots that caused them to:

- have unrealistic or unattainable goals
- work compulsively hard to the point of burnout
- drive others too hard
- have an insatiable need for recognition
- be power hungry
- need to seem perfect

If you have been accused of having any of these blind spots, pay attention. If someone has pointed these out to you in an annual review, in a side conversation, in an exit interview when you are the boss, or if your spouse has told you that any of these things is contributing to stress in your family life, take notice. These are symptoms not to be taken lightly. In fact, if someone has pointed any of these out to you, that person was doing you a favor. If you're trying to improve your EQ to improve your productivity and your chance of success, your blind spots will derail your progress in an instant.

Ways to Increase EQ

By having your EQ assessed you can pinpoint exactly where the gaps are so you can concentrate on the skills that will help you improve your EQ. Organizations that have EQ assessments done for all key leaders can also improve once they see the key leader profile. Once the organization knows where its gaps are, effort can be put into closing those gaps through training and by following through with key leaders to develop a Smart Zone environment.

In general, EQ can be increased with deliberateness and a commitment to continual reinforcement. Little skill will be developed if it is a one-shot pony training with little reinforcement from the decision makers and a lack of follow through.

Here are some Smart Ideas to increase your individual EQ:

- **Learn how to self-soothe.** When emotions are high, it is often difficult to calm yourself down so you can think more clearly. Some people are better than others at recovering to a more manageable level of emotions. You might try getting a better script for internal dialogue, exercising daily to manage stress, or learning how to talk yourself down when emotions are out of hand. Whatever works, do it.

- **Listen for cues in the words people use to help you know whether they are acting in a way that is cognitive (thinking) or emotional (feeling).** When someone says, "I feel the same way," they are more than likely responding emotionally. If the response is, "I see what you are saying," it may mean that the reaction is more cognitive in nature. It helps to be able to perceive the emotions of others, but even more important is being able to forecast if a conversation is going to get emotional by paying attention to the cues. When someone uses feeling words a lot, they are acting on a more emotional level. When someone uses words that are more cerebral and less emotional, it's likely that they are analyzing and thinking and are less likely to react emotionally. One is not better than the other, but it is always good to know the signals.

- **If you can't read another person's emotions, just ask.** It's not a crime to ask someone, "How do you feel about that?" Asking is better than trying to guess and then being wrong. Asking how someone feels about something and then really listening to the answer rather than to your question can help you be in the Smart Zone using your EQ skills.

Here are some Smart Ideas to increase your organization's EQ:

- **Make meetings productive.** Use people's energy and attention wisely. Send an agenda in advance that outlines who will report on what so that people can prepare. Allow people to attend only the parts of the meetings that involve them.

- **Be inclusive.** When you're speaking to a room of people, talk to everyone. Make eye contact with everyone, not just with those people whom you perceive as most important. Also be inclusive with your language. Not everyone is married, single, has children, etc. For example, instead of saying, "Everyone bring your spouse to the company picnic," say, "Please feel free to bring a guest to the company picnic." Also seek input from everyone and listen.

- **Create an environment where differences of opinion are emotionally safe.** Encourage others to voice their opinion in ways that challenge the discussion where appropriate. Even if the work environment does not allow open disagreement and differences of opinion, they will still be present, but in the destructive forms called "behind your back" and "under the table."

- **Create an optimistic and happy environment.** Have things that are fun and relaxing. As long as you aren't making fun of someone or something of value, having an inside or running joke about something helps encourage a healthy EQ. Every industry has its norm for what is appropriate in the work setting and what is not. A friend of mine at NBC decorated his office with bobble heads and other trinkets that he gathered from major news events. Because his office fit his personality and made sense for him, it was accepted. It was said that the higher-ups thought his office was the most annoying at NBC, but he was productive and well liked so it worked. In our clinical practice we have a running joke about a funky chicken and just having one around lightens the mood and creates an environment we all enjoy. One of the companies I worked with gave everyone a nickname. One man, who introduced himself as "Tuffy," told me even his customers called him by his nickname. Another person, whose

name is really Wendy at Aspen Achievement Group is affection-
ately called "Special Sauce."

- **Hire well.** If you've been relying on interview techniques, refer-
  ence checks, background checks, and drug testing to choose
  qualified candidates for jobs, you've been missing the boat.
  People leave organizations because of the boss, not because of the
  work. From the beginning recognize that more than just intelligence helps people be successful. Other traits that are people
  smart are more important for success.

These lists include just a few ideas of how you can increase your own
or your organization's EQ. By having your EQ assessed and learning
ways to close the gaps, you can improve your own EQ and ensure you're
Working in the Smart Zone.

Chapter Two
SMART Moves

- Figure out your funky chicken. Create an environment of optimism and happiness at work by having things that are fun and relaxing. As long as you aren't making fun of someone or something of value, having an inside or running joke about something helps level the playing field and encourage an environment with a healthy EQ.

- Being Emotionally Intelligent does *not* mean being more feminine in your thinking and in your actions. Emotional Intelligence is the ability to use emotions effectively. Research shows that our ability to manage our emotions and relationships with others is twice as important as our intelligence quotient (IQ).

- It's possible to improve your individual EQ. First, have your EQ assessed so you know where the gaps are, and then work on improving it. If you're not good at handling high emotions, start by finding a way to talk yourself down after a period of high emotions so you can think more clearly.

- Your organization can also improve its EQ. A simple way to start is to make meetings more productive and use people's energy and attention wisely. Send out an agenda in advance, and allow people to come just for their portion of the agenda. Another suggestion is to create an environment that welcomes differences of opinion.

Chapter 3

The Trust Factor

"There is nothing as fast as the speed of trust. There is nothing as profitable as the economics of trust. There is nothing as relevant as the pervasive impact of trust."
– Stephen M. R. Covey, CEO, CoveyLink

Become a Company That Outperforms

Trust is the second fundamental component in the Smart Zone model. Companies that build a climate of High Trust work in the Smart Zone.One of the foremost authorities on leadership and organizational development, Warren Bennis, believes that Trust is the lubrication that makes it possible for organizations to work.

The objective, hard data shows that companies with high trust outperform companies with low trust by nearly three times (Watson Wyatt's study, 2002).

Trust is Not an Agenda Item

Trust is the foundation of high-performing relationships. Trust is what allows the strategies in the Smart Zone model to be effective. Without the foundation of trust, even the best plans can fail.

Trust is not something that is a given just because you work together. Trust is not automatic for a group of people with common goals. Trust is not the result of a promotion. Trust is not an agenda item that you tell people they need to do. It is the accumulation of events that spontaneously appear and provide the opportunity for others to see what you are made of.

> Jim owned a small business, and most of his 40 employees had been with him since the business opened15 years before.Jim had a secret. He and his wife had been negotiating to sell the business in the new year. He didn't tell anyone, not even his loyal assistant Barbara, because he didn't want anything to jeopardize the deal. While he was tremendously loyal to the employees who had helped him build the company, he saw the sale of his business as a way for him and his wife to enjoy retirement.

Jim called me one evening in panic. Jim had just found out from his leadership staff that the bonus checks for his employees were bouncing. He was appalled this was happening just days before Christmas. His employees had received their annual bonus checks that afternoon with their regular paychecks, and he expected that most would be cashing their checks that day to cover Christmas expenses. He explained that the staff member responsible for transferring money in between accounts had delayed the transfer for some reason and there was now a hold, making it difficult to access either account. He couldn't just tell people to hold their checks another few days, and besides, would his employees believe that the money was there? Jim kept thinking about the timing of this with the possibility that he'd soon be announcing the sale of the business.

Jim felt doomed, and it was difficult for him to see his next step. He joked that he felt very out of his Smart Zone but that this was different than finding out you're wearing a pair of mismatched shoes. The consequences of this breach of trust were too high.

As I repeated to him that it was his responsibility to make it right, he stopped talking about his negative feelings for the staff person who'd made the mistake. At this point, the colorful adjectives he used to describe her were a distraction. He was able to get back to solution-oriented thinking and finally came up with a plan.

Jim transferred money from his private accounts and arranged to have all the bonus money paid in cash. At the bank the next morning, two loan officers helped him put the money in individual envelopes so he could hand deliver the bonuses to his employees before lunch. Jim walked up to his employees, one after the other, looked each of them in the eye, shook their hands and gave them their bonus money with a sincere apology. He told each one, "I couldn't get through the day without making sure you had this cash so you can go about your plans to provide for your family. I apologize for the inconvenience and for what this mistake is costing you."

At the end of the day, Jim was pleased that he'd made a wrong right. He knew the importance of taking matters into his own hands rather than being distracted by blaming others. He wanted his employees to know that he had their best interests at heart, even when he was planning to sell the business.

When the business was sold, none of the employees left. They wanted Jim to be happy and were loyal to his decision to retire. The new owners respected the importance of transferring the trust and were impressed with the way Jim had handled the situation. They were glad to do business with someone who could be trusted.

Trust is Not a Given

The Smart Zone model shows how Trust, along with EQ, has a major impact on the success of organizations. In his book, *The Speed of Trust*, Stephen M.R. Covey says that the following are present in a climate of distrust, eventually interfering with performance and the bottom line:

- Facts are manipulated or distorted
- Information and knowledge are withheld and hoarded
- People spin the truth to their advantage
- Getting the credit is very important
- New ideas are openly resisted and stifled
- Mistakes are covered up or covered over
- Most people are involved in a blame game, badmouthing others
- There is an abundance of "water cooler" talk
- There are numerous "meetings after the meetings"
- There are many "undiscussables"
- People tend to over-promise and under-deliver

*

- There are a lot of violated expectations for which people make many excuses
- People pretend bad things aren't happening or are in denial
- The energy level is low
- People often feel unproductive tension and sometimes even fear

In a Low Trust environment, strategies are less likely to be executed as planned. Employee turnover increases. Economic gains are lost. Double guessing decreases successful decision-making.

Covey believes that the seven High Trust dividends are:
1. Increased value
2. Accelerated growth
3. Enhanced innovation
4. Improved collaboration
5. Stronger partnering
6. Better execution
7. Heightened loyalty

The following scenario shows how Trust can be challenged early in working relationships and how managing perceptions and communication can suffer too.

> In Zan's first week in her job for an international elevator company, one of the high-rise buildings in downtown San Antonio, Texas called her to set up a special move on the freight elevator over the upcoming weekend. They needed to move a large refrigerator on the top of the elevator cab (because it was too large to fit inside the elevator) up to a restaurant on the 33rd floor, and requested the work be done on Sunday when no one else in the building would need the freight elevator. When Zan received the request she contacted the weekend duty mechanics to set up the work.

On Monday morning Bill, the regular route mechanic for the high-rise building, showed up at her desk. "Don't do things behind my back," he barked. Zan was puzzled. "I heard you had the weekend duty guys do a move over the weekend. I don't like people sneaking around my back!"

Zan immediately apologized. "I'm sorry, it didn't occur to me to tell you about it because you weren't on call this weekend. I thought you'd appreciate me not bothering you with it."

Zan perceived that she was helping Bill by not bothering him with the request for weekend work. Bill perceived that Zan was setting up work behind his back. They each perceived the situation differently.

Zan also learned an important lesson in communication. Everyone likes to know what's going on when it pertains to them and their job. Bill felt ownership in his work at the high-rise building and, out of respect for Bill, Zan owed him an explanation for the work she had scheduled.

The Many Forms of Trust

Trust is not just about relationships with people. There are also other kinds of trust:

- **Brand Trust:** Remember the Tylenol scare and the *E. coli* outbreak at Jack in the Box? Both companies had to work hard to regain brand trust once their reputations were violated. Think of the brands you trust. Some that may come to mind are Band-Aid brand bandages, Toyota, Starbucks, and Hewlett-Packard. In our office we trust Office Depot, UniBall Pens, and Corner Bakery.

- **Self-Trust:** We hear of so many companies who hire consultants and pay big bucks for help with advertising campaigns, branding development, and even office decoration. There is a perception (or misperception) that the experts know best when it comes to advertising, building a brand, or decorating your office. A gut feeling might tell you that the experts are not on the right track, but when you don't trust yourself, you might succumb to the belief that the expert knows better. Learn to trust your gut and yourself; your instincts are better than you think. Be more decisive and listen to your intuition and what is really important to you to build your level of self-trust. I call this honoring your non-negotiable necessities—those things that you value and believe that when you honor them, you build self-trust.

- **Relationship Trust:** Both at work and at home, relationships require trust to grow and develop. This kind of trust is what most people think of in discussions of trust. While relationship trust is the most common and most recognizable, when it's shaken you can be knocked out of your Smart Zone. Ask yourself if you are trustworthy in relationships both at work and at home.

- **Organizational Trust:** Employees want assurances that their organizations will take care of them when they've been loyal and productive. When the economy is poor, business decisions will center on improving the bottom line. Businesses focus on positions and eliminating waste rather than on who is liked. When Radio Shack employees were laid off through email, that was an example of poor organizational trust. When school systems run out of money and educational value goes down, trust is disrupted. Do you trust your organization? Do you contribute your best so that your organization can be trusted?

Building the Platform of Trust

The platform of Trust is attainable in any relationship at work and at home, and there are also ways to keep it steady and strong. The following Smart Ideas can strengthen the platform of Trust and allow you to Work in the Smart Zone:

- **Address and right the wrongs.** Blaming others is one of the fastest ways to burn yourself in the trust department. Passing the buck shows that you lack integrity. Do what is necessary, even when it inconveniences you. If it's your responsibility, fix it. If you knock something off someone's desk, pick it up! Do you believe I even have to say something so obvious? Taken to the extreme this principle means managing what's on your watch. Remember Jim, the business owner who covered the bonus checks with his own money to right the wrong? That's an example of the ultimate in building trust.

- **Be loyal to others when they're not present.** At work, your alliances may change, and someone who's your peer today could be your supervisor or manager tomorrow. People will trust you when they have confidence that you can be trusted when they're not present, and that may not happen until they experience you behind the backs of others.Don't gossip, don't speak for other people, and encourage communication between two people instead of triangulating yourself into the communication of others. In this world of technology, there are many ways to maintain healthy alliances to build trust.

- **Be clear with expectations and hold people accountable.** When supervising people, be deliberate about the outcomes you are expecting and when possible, make them measurable. Set timelines so you can hold people accountable and monitor whether or not they have the self-management skills to hold themselves accountable.

- **Build your self-regard.** Self-regard is how you see yourself and how others see you. It is very different than self-esteem. Your self-regard is what lets people know whether they can trust you to accept feedback, manage criticism, and be honest with them in return. If you're working on increasing your EQ you're also building your self-regard so that people can be confident that they can be honest with you. Self-regard also considers the bad as well as the good.

- **Be predictable, caring, and faithful.** When you're predictable, others begin to see that you are consistent. When you're genuinely caring, others will trust you and see you as compassionate and invested in them. When you're faithful, you build loyalty, which is the result of a trusting relationship.

- **Demonstrate respect for those you work with.** One-sided respect in relationships is temporary and delicate, yet over time it builds into respect that is reciprocal.

- **Follow through on your commitments.** People can smell insincerity when a commitment is not followed through. When someone gets the reputation that he or she can't be trusted to do as they say, they face a hard uphill climb. The old saying, "under promise and over deliver," holds true even among co-workers.

- **Be the same in public and in private.** Some people are better at acting than others. It's better to be transparent than to be fake. When people can count on you being the same in private as you are in public, they'll trust you to be who you say you are. They'll also trust that what you say today will be consistent with what you say tomorrow.

Trust is one of the most important components in building a Smart Zone community. Without trust, the benefits of building high EQ cannot be sustained, and the strategies that lead to productivity will be sabotaged. Trust provides the platform for productivity, efficiency and for *Working in the Smart Zone.*

Chapter Three
SMART Moves

- Trust and EQ both have a major impact on the success of organizations. Research shows that companies with High Trust outperform companies with Low Trust by nearly three times.

- It's possible to build and strengthen the trust in your relationships at home and at work. One way to do that is to follow through on your commitments so that people know they can rely on you. Also, be loyal to others when they're not present. They'll be much more likely to do the same for you.

- Trust is one of the most important components in building a Smart Zone community. Without trust your organization cannot sustain the other gains it makes, such as in building EQ and improving productivity.

Chapter 4

Managing Perception

"There has been much tragedy in my life.
At least half of it actually happened."
– Mark Twain

Worry is the Mismanagement of Perceptions

The first strategy in the Smart Zone model is about managing perception. We all tend to misperceive, especially when emotions are high. At work non-verbal cues can be misread. When there is fear there is a tendency to read between the lines.

One of my favorite definitions of worry is:

"Worry is the misuse of imagination."
– Audrey Woodhall

When we are not managing our perceptions we are abusing our imaginations. Sometimes it happens that two people get the same memo, hear the same announcement, see the same picture, and read the same email, and yet perceive the same information very differently. When this happens it's important to be able to manage your perception, and more important, to allow yourself to be influenced while taking steps to influence others.

What Organizations Value

Organizations value those who are able to manage their perceptions and be open to the perceptions of others.

Jill and Randy had both worked in the banking industry for almost 15 years, and had seen the industry change. Sometimes the change was for the better; sometimes it was for the worse. Last fall a new CEO was brought in to build their customer base in the competitive market in southern Arizona.

Jill and Randy were both given the opportunity to meet with the new CEO individually, so they both stayed late to prepare quarterly numbers for the meeting scheduled for the next morning. As Randy stopped by

Jill's office to say goodbye, he casually asked Jill what she thought of the new CEO.

Jill gave him a rave review, describing him as friendly, approachable, interested, and knowledgeable. She told Randy how comfortable she was with this new CEO coming on board.

Randy laughed out loud. "Are you sure you met with the same person today as I did?" He was so dumbfounded that he even asked her to tell him what the CEO was wearing.

Randy described the CEO as remote, aloof, uninterested, and flighty. His perception was that the new CEO was clueless about their industry, their unique challenges, and the potential for growth in their region. As Randy and Jill talked further, she attempted to persuade him that he was being too judgmental about the CEO.

What was the reason for the discrepancy? Randy and the previous CEO had been buddies, so when he left the bank Randy expected the worst. Jill, on the other hand, welcomed new leadership and believed that new blood was needed take their business to the next level. Randy was willing to listen to Jill's perceptions of the new CEO, and as a result he left the building with an adjusted, more optimistic attitude about the potential for success. Because Randy was able to manage his perceptions and allowed himself to be influenced by Jill's impressions he will be more likely to benefit from the new CEO's influence.

Common Misperceptions at Work

Certain misperceptions are common in work environments. These misperceptions need to be identified and managed successfully:

- You need to spend money to make money
- Longer hours equal higher productivity

- The loudest voice is always right
- Asking for help is a sign of weakness
- You must be physically in the office to be productive
- Leaders have all the answers
- The old way is always the best way
- I already know everything I need to
- The leadership doesn't know what is going on
- The leadership is "not in charge"
- We know the product or purpose
- My role is not important
- We don't have to pay attention to the competition
- Everyone should have the same workstyle
- The budget isn't important
- The company "owes" me
- We can't afford to lose someone
- Change is bad
- Only one person can do/accomplish a task
- Your opinion doesn't matter, won't count or be listened to

Strategies to Manage Perceptions at Work

Here are some Smart Ideas to help you manage your perceptions:

- **Listen first.** Remember that other people's perceptions are different from yours. See those as opportunities to exercise your ability to manage your perceptions.

- **Learn techniques to influence others.** Don't be afraid to say that you see things differently. Participate in healthy discussion, which is different than conflict. Many times healthy discussion paves the way for new ideas and better ways of doing things.

- **Create a work environment that promotes discussion of differences in perception.** In meetings, ask questions: "Who sees this differently? Let's think this idea through completely" and

"What would our competition say?" Invite others to challenge ideas and listen when they do so.

- **Avoid email as a way to challenge the perceptions of others.** Discussions of perceptual differences are always best done in person.

- **Take responsibility for your misperceptions.** Don't be afraid to admit when you've seen something from a different angle and are now willing to change your mind. It isn't about admitting you are wrong; for some people that's just too hard to do. It's about being able to tell someone that you appreciate how they helped you change your perception. Now that won't hurt to do.

You constantly need to manage your perceptions so that you can tune into how you perceive and how you can influence and be influenced by others. It's important to manage your perceptions rather than set yourself up to have your perceptions continually challenged. Perceptions are personal, but they influence individuals and organizations emotionally, intellectually, and behaviorally as you are *Working in the Smart Zone*.

SMART Moves

- We all have a tendency to misperceive, especially when emotions are high. It's important that you constantly manage your perception so that you can tune into how you perceive, how you can influence others, and how they can influence you.

- Remember that others have different perceptions, so listen first. Learn techniques to influence others. Invite a healthy discussion on your differences in perception, and avoid using email to challenge others' perceptions. These discussions should always be handled in person.

- Take responsibility for your misperceptions. It's okay to admit that you've seen a situation from a different angle and have now changed your mind. It isn't about admitting you're wrong; it's about being able to tell someone that you appreciate how they helped you change your perception.

Chapter 5

Communication

"You can't build a reputation on what you are going to do."
– Henry Ford

Communicating with Emotional Competency

There is research that top performing sales clerks are 12 times more productive than those at the bottom and 85% more productive than an average performer. About 1/3 of this difference is due to technical skill and cognitive ability while 2/3 is due to emotional competence (Goleman, 1998).

Every profession, not just sales positions, can learn from this information. We can all communicate with emotional competency. When we do so, we outperform those who are focused on technical skill and cognitive ability.

> It was the first cold day of the season and I was preparing for a late-morning flight from Dallas to Houston for a consultation. Since I had the luxury of taking my time in the morning I spent some time with my children as they got ready for school. Because it was the first cold day they were unwilling to wear their typical shorts and t-shirts. If they'd had their way they would have worn their ski gear just for the car ride through the carpool line. With almost simultaneous glee all three boys came out from their rooms wearing jeans that resembled capri pants. Some of you would call these high waters. As we mauled the collective jean collection it was clear that the boys were without jeans that would fit. As they went off to school in sweatpants, I realized I had time to stop at SuperTarget and buy them new jeans on my way to the airport.
>
> SuperTarget can be counted on to be your one-stop shop for groceries, clothing, household items, and everything you need and can't live without. I have always had a good experience at SuperTarget so it made sense to stop there. This particular morning I was one of the first people to walk through the doors. I knew it was my lucky day when I saw the abundant supply of

slim-sized jeans in the jean aisle. I grabbed as many as I could in the sizes our boys needed. Because I'd made good time, I took a few minutes to pick up other things I'd been meaning to get. With my cart pretty full, I made my way to the checkout aisles.

As I placed my items on the moving belt, I was greeted by a friendly cashier named Jennifer. Once all of my items were out of the cart I started to worry that I hadn't been cautious about what I was spending. Jennifer congratulated me on hitting the mother lode of slim jeans. She asked me if I was there because the morning's cold spell had made me realize that my children needed the right size pants. We both laughed as we compared the terms for high waters. She said her children were also clothing challenged that morning. At that point I felt as if Jennifer knew me—that she knew my life.

As we continued to talk about how I got more than I expected, Jennifer told me she could save me some money on my purchase. At this point I was so engaged in the conversation with Jennifer that I felt she was actually trying to do me a favor. She said she could save me at least $15 quickly and easily. As I pondered whether she was talking about a coupon, she told me that signing up for a SuperTarget credit card today would give me 10% off my purchases. At that point I stopped dead in my tracks because the last thing I wanted was a credit card.

I told Jennifer that I wasn't interested in the card and that I was in a hurry, but she suggested that I sign up for the card, take advantage of the 10% cash back, and then never use the card again. Jennifer had re-engaged my interest. I knew I was self disciplined enough to benefit this one time and then cut up the credit card once it arrived in the mail. At that point I was back feeling as if she was doing me a favor. It felt like she had anticipated my concerns because she had an acceptable answer every time.

I was getting worried about getting to the airport, so I told her that I didn't think I had time to complete a lengthy application. With that she made my life even easier; she asked me for my phone number, and instantly a computer-generated short form appeared. Within a minute I'd signed up to become a member of the SuperTarget credit card family. Before I even put my pen away Jennifer handed me $15 in crisp bills, which I immediately wanted to spend at SuperTarget.

Finally, as I gathered my packages Jennifer gave me a bonus proposition: the 10% cash back offer was good all day long at any Target store. As I made my way to the parking lot I actually wondered if the person picking me up at the airport in Houston would mind stopping at SuperTarget so I could continue my buying spree.

By using the skill of emotional competence to communicate effectively, Jennifer made me feel like a winner. I felt she was looking out for me, wanting me to succeed. Think about how you usually hear the credit card proposition—a person with a clipboard approaches and asks if you'd like to save 10% by opening up a credit card. Naturally, a full cart invites the most solicitations. The clipboard communicator uses technical and cognitive ability to communicate. In response to this approach you think, "What's 10% anyway?" and maybe you focus on the words "credit card," which tend to have negative connotations. Jennifer's approach was more effective because she communicated by building a relationship. She was successful even though our interaction was brief. She thought beyond the 10% and anticipated the value to me, making me listen to what she had to say.

In your work environment do you use emotional competence to communicate? If you're an unsuccessful communicator maybe it's because you rely on technical and cognitive ability. These fact-based methods of communication are limiting because they do not create a relationship with other people. When you talk about 10%, that is math. When you talk about being a "winner" because you found slim jeans, that is based on emotional competency. When you talk about the 50 reasons why someone should sign up for a credit card, that requires thought in the form of pros and cons. When you talk about how it is easy and smart to sign up for a credit card, that creates an environment where people feel good about themselves. Talking from a position of emotional competency creates a path to the Smart Zone.

Communicating with Trust

Communicating with Trust is also a key component of the Smart Zone Model. While organizations are building High Trust environments it's actually very easy to instill a sense of trust in those working together. Here are some communication methods that will build a High Trust Smart Zone environment:

Typical Communication	High Trust Communication
"I'd like you to do this part of this project."	"I have confidence in your ability to do this part of the project."
"You are going to need some help to get this done."	"You deserve to have help getting this done."
"This is an important project and will require a lot of work."	"We chose you because this is an important project and will require a lot of work."
"People who succeed here are the ones who work hard."	"I'm confident you will succeed here because you work hard."
"I want you on this project."	"I have confidence in you being on this project."

Do People Want to Communicate and Do Business With You?

When I shop at SuperTarget, I'm doing business with Jennifer. To me Jennifer *is* SuperTarget because she creates an experience where I feel like a winner. I feel that somebody is looking out for me.

In your business, do clients do business with *you*, or are you just what they get because you've answered the phone? Do you provide value? Are you building relationships in the way you communicate? Or are you just giving facts, hoping that communicating with intellect will get you far? Are you the face of your company? Are you the service or product your company provides?

Fast forward through a few more SuperTarget trips. One day I'm there with my boys and by this point Jennifer and our family are on a first-name basis. When Jennifer sees I'm wearing a University of Florida sweatshirt she excitedly asks me if I'm from Florida. This is where it gets weird as I wonder what connection we have. She explains she's from Orlando. I tell her I grew up in Clearwater. When I ask her what she did in Orlando, her answer doesn't surprise me. Jennifer was Snow White at Disney World.

Snow White works at SuperTarget at Park and the Dallas North Tollway in Plano, Texas. Think about it. Snow White has to communicate with emotional intelligence. Snow White is not allowed to have a bad day. She has to be able to sense feelings when children approach her with ambivalence. She is the symbol for EQ and *Working in the Smart Zone*.

Be Snow White in Your Organization

Do you strive to communicate with emotional competence, or are you still relying on the limitations of technical and cognitive ability? How can you communicate like Snow White? Try these Smart Ideas:

- **Use non-verbal communication to engage with the other person**. Give your full attention to the person you're communicating with. Even though you're in the middle of something else, stop what you're doing, turn away from the computer or put down your BlackBerry, turn towards the person and make eye contact.

- **Minimize distractions when you're talking to someone else**. If you have to respond to a distraction, do it in a productive way. For example, if your cell phone goes off while you're talking to someone at work, say, "Excuse me just a minute. I want to make sure it's not the call from the bookkeeping department I've been waiting for." Then, check the caller ID, and if you see it isn't the call you're expecting, smile back at the person and say, "I can call them back when you and I are done talking," and continue your conversation. If you see that it's a call you must take gracefully say, "This is the call I have been waiting for. I need to take it. If you don't mind, give me just a second and then I'd like to get right back to what you and I were talking about. I don't want to end our conversation right now if that is okay." This will make the person recognize that your communication with him or her is important.

- **When you want to influence another person, pay attention to the cues in the conversation or in what the person is doing and listen to what is important in their communication.** You are way out of your Smart Zone when you ask a question the person just answered (shows you weren't listening) or you get mixed up when you respond. When a person has to correct details you should already know, you lose tremendous credibility and lose your opportunity to influence.

- **Always call the person by their first name when you're first communicating.** This creates familiarity, and almost everyone enjoys hearing their name said in a friendly manner.

- **Don't force yourself on the person if he or she appears to be in no mood to communicate.** A child would never be able to bond with a Snow White who was too forward. If deadlines permit, when you need to talk with a co-worker but you sense the timing is bad, ask if the person would like to talk in a few minutes about the project and give permission to reconnect later. Make it okay to follow up when the person is more prepared to receive your communication. By sensing that the person is preoccupied or not ready to connect, you are practicing your EQ skills. There are times you won't have this luxury, but recognize that sometimes forcing the issue will likely be unproductive.

- **When a person seems apprehensive, focus your communication on what you *can* do for him or her rather than on the 50 reasons why he or she is wrong.** Be decisive so you communicate confidence. Don't over promise but do earn credibility by being firm about your beliefs of what you can provide.

- **Be relevant in your communication.** People do business with people they like, and being relevant is one of the ways people are likeable. Relevance is your ability to connect with the interests, wants, and needs of other people.

- **Talk about "value" when you communicate with other people.** Don't just give them all the facts. When you are communicating a work issue, a solution to a problem, or how to get ready to present an idea, whenever possible include in your communication the value to the person or the issue.

Communication is about more than words; it's about relationships. Communication is a tool that keeps you *Working in the Smart Zone*, building value in relationships and in organizations to increase the bottom line.

SMART Moves

- Strive to communicate with emotional competence so that you build a relationship with the person. Communicating facts using your technical and cognitive abilities is ineffective. Focus on communicating value so that people will want to do business with you.

- Non-verbal communication is an important part of communicating with emotional competence. Make eye contact, minimize distractions, use their first name, and give the person your full attention. These methods all help people feel that your communication with them is important.

- Communicating is a two-way street. Listening is just as crucial as talking. Pay attention to both the verbal and non-verbal cues in the conversation so that you know what's important to the other person.

Chapter 6

Solution Oriented

"None of us is as smart as all of us."
– Japanese proverb

Problem Solving in the Smart Zone

In our personal lives we are used to solving problems on our own or with an informal network. But at work, problem solving requires collaboration. Embrace the fact that your team at work has the capability to solve problems of great magnitude.

Problems in the workplace come in all shapes and sizes, so there is no magic all-purpose formula for solving every problem we encounter. We must adapt our problem solving process to fit the problem at hand, which requires both cognitive and emotional skills. Toward this end, here are five Smart Ideas for problem solving in the Smart Zone:

- **Make sure the problem can be solved.** Is there really a problem and if so, is it solvable? For example, if your problem is that the sky is blue, then you may need to rethink the problem. In a recent issue of *Fast Company*, Jochen Zeitz, CEO of the shoe-maker Puma, said, "Design usually starts with 'There is no way' and then we say, 'Okay, how can we make this work?'"

- **Define the problem in one sentence.** This sounds easy but is really quite difficult. A well-defined problem makes the solved state more measurable. Charles Kettering, co-holder of more than 140 patents and inventor of such things as the spark plug, leaded gasoline and Freon for refrigerators and air conditioners, once said, "A problem well stated is a problem half solved."

- **Focus on the solved state.** Ask yourself and your team these questions:
  1. How will we know when the problem has been solved?
  2. What does the solved state look and feel like?
  3. What is tangible evidence that the problem is solved?

- **Use a problem solving technique that works for your group.** There are several problem solving techniques, including brain-storming, root-cause analysis, and the drill down technique. One technique that might be appropriate is the appreciation technique, which is a powerful way to extract the maximum amount

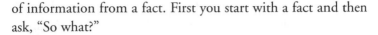

of information from a fact. First you start with a fact and then ask, "So what?"

Example:

Our warehouse does not have the required part in stock.

So what?

The part will need to be ordered from a vendor.

So what?

It will take more time to get the needed part.

So what?

Our customer will need to be notified of the delay.

So...

In the future, we need a process for the warehouse to order parts in advance so parts will not be out of stock when needed.

Although you may come up with the same conclusion without a formal technique, this approach provides a framework for extracting information quickly and reliably.

- **Develop an accountability plan.** Many problem solving sessions end when the solution is determined. But wait! Go one more step and assign specific action items to people with a time frame for completion. Design a way to hold those responsible for the solution accountable for the results.

Problem Focused or Solution Oriented?

How you approach the problem will determine how others respond—as problem focused or solution oriented.

> Sandy had been a terrible employee. She was often late, wrote personal emails on company time, and lived in a fantasy world. She still thought about her high school boyfriend, even though she was 42, had been married for many years and had three children. Her boss, a conservative man named Charles, was preparing for her performance review, and knew he had to change his approach. He had talked with Sandy in the past about

her inappropriate use of company time and had told her she shared too much personal information, making her colleagues uncomfortable.

The mistake Charles had made in the past was asking Sandy "why" questions, which only encouraged conversations that focused on the problem. This approach took Charles out of his Smart Zone. He would ask her:

> *"Why do you spend so much time answering personal email?"*

And Sandy would answer:

> *"My internet at home isn't working but I can't figure out if something's wrong with my computer or if it's our service. I tried to call the internet provider but I spent SO LONG on hold. But my husband doesn't see why we need it and he says the kids just waste time on the internet anyway. So I only have the internet at work, and besides, it only takes me a few minutes to answer personal email. I try to do it on my break time."*

Then Charles would ask:

> *"Why were you late to the staff meeting?"*

And Sandy's response was:

> *"My son had trouble finding his homework for school and I helped him look for it. By the time we got to school I had to go inside and sign him in since they considered him tardy. Once I got in my car, I realized I needed to get gas so I had to stop and there was this big line. Then the traffic—the TRAFFIC—was so bad that it took me forever to get here and by that time I couldn't find a parking space."*

Charles:

> *"Why do you talk so much about your personal business?"*

Sandy:

> *"I don't talk more about personal business than anyone else. Janet tells us all about her sex life and how she thinks her husband is cheating on her and Jeff talks all the time about his money problems. Why am I getting in trouble when everyone else is doing the same thing?"*

Charles:

> *"Why don't you use your time more effectively?"*

Sandy:

> *"I do use my time effectively. I do everything you tell me to do. Just yesterday you gave me a project and said it might take me two days and I finished it in one day. If I was wasting time would I have had it on your desk yesterday? Tell me that!"*

Are you exhausted yet?

Asking "why" questions gets people talking about the problem, which is exhausting to listen to.

Get Talking About the Solution

Instead of asking "why," ask "what" and "how" questions, which will get people talking about the solution. In the questions that Charles asked of Sandy, changing the "why" to "what" and "how" questions would make all the difference in moving forward to talking about solutions.

Problem Focused Question	Solution Oriented Question
"Why do you spend so much time answering personal email?"	"What other options do you have to write personal emails so you don't do it on company time?"
"Why were you late to the staff meeting?"	"What do you need to do to make sure that you are on time to staff meetings all the time?"
"Why do you talk so much about your personal business?"	"How can you make sure you and the other people in your department talk about personal business outside of company time?"
"Why don't you use your time more effectively?"	"How much extra time do you have to help me on some important projects?"

Working in the Smart Zone is about being solution oriented rather than problem focused. Organizations that are solution oriented can elicit the best from each employee to create a climate of Smart Zone thinking. This will boost productivity and contribute to the bottom line and keep you *Working in the Smart Zone.*

Chapter Six
SMART Moves

- One of the most important stages in problem solving is defining the problem. A well-defined problem makes the solved state more measurable.

- Don't forget to develop an accountability plan after you've come up with the solution. Assign specific action items and set a time frame for completion. Design a way to hold those responsible for the solution accountable for the results.

- How you approach a problem will determine how other people respond—as problem focused or solution oriented. If you ask "why" questions, you'll get answers that focus on the problem. Instead, ask "how" and "what" to get answers that focus on the solution.

Chapter 7

Managing Stress

"Never let urgent crowd out the important."
– Kelly Catlin Walker

Shaking the Work Debris

Managers and executives who work long hours often tell me that at the end of the day, it's difficult to shake the feeling of being at work. Even when they get home they don't feel "at home." They feel disconnected and preoccupied with what took place during the workday or are anticipating the problems of the next day.

Part of the issue is that typically the intensity during our workdays is different than the intensity of our home lives. Although our home and work lives both take considerable mental and physical energy we still have to shift gears when we walk in the door at home.

Leaving Stress at the Office

Because we provide strategies for improving productivity at home and work, we hear a lot about how stress bleeds into all areas of life. By being in the Smart Zone your productivity is maximized. Here are three Smart Ideas for leaving stress at the office:

- **Set aside 10 minutes after lunch to return personal phone calls.** This will eliminate your need to talk on your cell phone on the drive home at the end of the day. Instead you can listen to good music or an audio book.

- **Carve out transition time.** Devote the final hours of your workday to some of your least-pressured tasks. You will feel a sense of accomplishment by completing at least one thing before day's end. But what about the days when there are no low-pressure tasks and you haven't accomplished a thing? Then use this time to make a list for the following day in your electronic schedule or on paper so that you don't have to tell yourself, "I won't forget. I'll do it tomorrow." Eliminate the need to keep work tasks on your mind. If a task is on the list it will be waiting on you in the morning. Free up your mind to relax and enjoy your evening.

- **Put work on the back burner.** When you walk in the door at home resist the urge to immediately start talking about your day.

Cooper and Sawaf, authors of *Executive EQ,* call this time a "transitional buffer zone." This is time to renew your spirit by being home. Don't run to your computer to return emails. You might first greet your family, listen to your family tell you about their day, and change into more comfortable clothes.

What about just coping with daily stressors and those stressors that result from the pressure of deadlines, poor work relationships, and feeling like you just can't cut it? Most of us have heard about counting to 10 and taking a breath. Most of the people we see in our consulting practice tell us those strategies are ineffective. Let's take a look at stress management another way, a smarter way; one that involves shifting the way you think. When you change the way you think, your actions will follow.

The Bucket Theory of Stress

I believe everybody has a bucket of stress inside of them. When something causes stress, frustrates you, makes you angry, or just requires a lot of attention and energy, the bucket starts to fill. It's important to be aware of how full your bucket is, because when it fills up completely, people have what I call an exaggerated response.

An exaggerated response is when you overreact to whatever the trigger is at the time. You know you're having an exaggerated response when people look at you like you are weird or out of control, or tell you continually to calm down and ask why you are getting so upset, and try and convince you that the stressor is not worth your reaction. Then you start to realize you are wigging out or, as some kids call it, "losing it." Typically when your bucket is full, even small things can trigger an exaggerated response. Perhaps the copy machine jams while you're trying to make a few copies. You aren't even in a hurry to get the copies done but because your bucket is full you don't have any room for tolerance and you're likely to overreact. If your bucket weren't full, the situation might not be so aggravating.

I believe most people don't know when their bucket is full. To decrease tension at work and at home, it would be important to know. There are many everyday things that can fill your bucket: training a new secretary, worries about catching your flight, a looming deadline, learning new software, or trying to lose 20 pounds. Sometimes we can anticipate when our buckets will get full. For me, even getting ready for a party at our house can fill my bucket. If you can anticipate something that will fill your bucket, you can get ahead of it.

Here are other things that tend to fill people's buckets:

- a long commute to work
- being asked to do more at work with fewer resources
- being sick
- daily decisions about finances
- environmental stressors
- difficult relationships
- disagreements with employees
- disagreements with your spouse
- being up for a promotion
- learning a new skill

When I talk to corporations or at conferences about *Working in the Smart Zone* I hear a lot of great ideas for emptying your bucket. While some of you may think it is enough to just reduce the level it so the bucket doesn't overflow, it is a better idea to work to keep the level low most of the time. Sometimes that means you have to empty your bucket more often. This approach means more than "don't sweat the small stuff." It is recognizing when you have what I call "stress kindling," where you continually add to your bucket, a little bit at a time. Over time, it adds up and your bucket is full. Some suggestions include the following:

- getting enough sleep
- exercising
- spending quality time with family
- spending quality time with friends
- getting involved in a community of faith
- getting involved in community groups or activities
- meditating and doing yoga
- reading
- staying organized

Some of these stress management tactics can even become an activity or focus in your department at work. You might consider some of the following activities, which I've heard are being done in other organizations:

- Join Weight Watchers together and go to meetings at lunch.

- Start a book club for business books.

- Start a book club for self-help books or for fiction.

- Organize a community service project that fits the passion of your department, and get your whole family involved.

- Identify a value of the month (example: the Smart Zone philosophy of asking "what" and "how" instead of "why") and display it in a central location.

Adopt a cause during the holidays and instead of having a company party get involved with that organization's events, and maybe even play Santa. Be hands on and learn to take the focus off of yourself. These are things that change lifestyles and bond people together.

Finally, if you sense a co-worker is stressed, it's much better to say, "Your bucket is full. Let's figure out a way to empty it," rather than, "What is wrong with you? Can't you handle it?" In search of temporary relief, people in your workplace may make poor choices to try to empty their buckets, but I believe some of these things might eventually be recycled, and go on to quickly fill those buckets to the brim.

Some of the poor choices for emptying your bucket can include:

- affairs

- alcohol abuse

- substance abuse (illegal and prescription)

- excessive withdrawal from social activities and groups

- smoking

- stealing

- gambling

- gossip

- overeating

Is There Such a Thing as Good Stress?

Yes. Good stress, or Eustress, motivates you to action, helping you focus and getting your adrenaline pumping to bring passion and excitement to whatever you are doing.

How you perceive a stressful event is determined by how you think about it. By recognizing the opportunity in any stressful event, you can motivate yourself to use it productively, making it a good stress that can benefit you.

Think

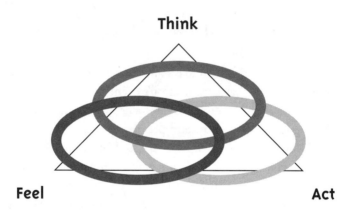

Feel　　　　　　　　　　　　　　　**Act**

The way you think affects the way you feel, which affects the way you act. The way you feel affects the way you think, which affects the way you act. The way you act affects the way you think, which affects the way you feel.

And so on. You have control over whether you are experiencing good stress or bad. If you want your body to age, wear down, or fail you, then think, feel, and act as if all stress is bad. On the other hand, if you want to work in the Smart Zone, think, feel, and act as if stress is good and motivates you to do your best. Stress doesn't define you when you are in the Smart Zone.

Redefine Yourself

Beginning in 2008 I am promising myself and telling people around me that I no longer want the words "busy" and "Susan" to be together in the same sentence. Wouldn't that be great? It's up to me and it takes redefining myself. I'd much rather have the words "productive," "kind," "fun," and "smart" describe me. If I *think* busy and *feel* busy then I will *act* busy instead of productive, kind, fun, and smart.

I've had to change my vocabulary so I do not automatically answer questions with explanations of all that we have going on. I also have the opportunity to redefine myself to show my other attributes. Think about one word people might use to describe you that you might want to change. Here are some descriptions that I would think might need to be changed:

- unapproachable
- immature
- unprofessional
- unreliable
- unmanageable
- not a team player
- selfish
- unpopular
- irresponsible
- flaky
- dingy
- self absorbed

Stress isn't just about counting to 10 or walking away. Understanding how you contribute to stress, how you prepare for it, and how you react to it will allow you to continue *Working in the Smart Zone*.

Chapter Seven
SMART Moves

- Value your time at work and at home. At the end of the workday today make a list of what you'd like to accomplish after today and put it out of your mind until tomorrow.

- Learn to recognize when your bucket of stress is full, and what kind of things cause it to fill up. If you can anticipate what fills your bucket you can get ahead of it. Most important, though, find a few effective ways that will help you empty your bucket. Perhaps you need more exercise, more sleep, or more activities with family and friends.

- You have control over whether you're experiencing good stress or bad. Thinking, acting and feeling that all stress is bad will quickly age you, but thinking, acting and feeling as if stress is good will motivate you to do your best, and put you in the Smart Zone.

- Benefit your whole department by getting everyone involved in stress management activities. Consider taking on a community service project together, adopting a cause around the holidays, or joining Weight Watchers.

Chapter 8

Mental Theater

*"The greater danger for most of us is not that our aim is too high
and we miss it, but that it is too low and we reach it."*
– Michelangelo

Negative Drama Out

When we attempt to manage our perceptions and take responsibility for them, it's important to recognize we can create a "drama" in our heads so it seems as if the event actually happened. We call this "Mental Theater."

- In a work environment, a manager may perceive that his boss is upset with him because he doesn't look him in the eye when they're talking. So the manager then proceeds to relate to his boss as if there really was a disagreement.

- An assistant may believe that a co-worker who is whispering is talking about her behind her back. The assistant then becomes hostile as if there has been a breach of trust.

- A wife may believe that her husband is having an affair because he is too friendly with the attractive woman next door. She then begins to treat him as if he's been unfaithful.

If there's a negative drama playing out in your mind, and yet you never address it, then you have developed a destructive form of Mental Theater.

Filling in the Middle Parts

When we have only part of the story, we tend to fill in the other parts. Think of how you put together a puzzle. Most of us separate the end pieces of the puzzle from those that go in the middle. We hold up the picture on the box top and try to figure out which end pieces go where. What if we don't have the box top and we only have half of the picture? What if we only have half of the story?

One evening while we waited to be seated for dinner at a local restaurant we sat trying to piece together a puzzle that was lying on top of the table. There was no box top and we had no idea what the puzzle was supposed to be. Almost all the pieces were black with a few showing signs of some kind of white strip. Was it a dark sky? Was it a dark road? Only later we found out that the picture was a box of Oreo cookies. Without that picture we might never have figured out where the pieces fit. We were wasting a lot of time trying to figure out what we were making.

When we only know one piece of information about a situation, we tend to try and fill in the blanks so that the situation makes sense for us. Have you ever felt that way at work? Have you ever had only a small piece of information and you had to try and figure out the rest?

Sam thought that he'd get the opportunity to work on the Fabor account. He'd been with the company for more than 15 years and he expected that the biggest account landed this year would come to him as project manager. Instead, the account went to Wendy. This was a complete surprise to Sam and he wondered why his boss gave the account to Wendy instead of to him.

Feeling very frustrated and slighted, Sam talked to his wife about how angry he was and how he resented Wendy for getting the account, but he wasn't sure what to do. He didn't want to be a whiner but he believed that he needed to address the situation with someone. He knew that he shouldn't talk about his frustration with other co-workers but he just couldn't hide his anger.

Sam decided to talk with Wendy about the situation. He knew that talking to his boss would only make him look like he wasn't a team player. After all, it was his boss' decision to give it to Wendy.

After talking to Wendy, he felt better and could see that Wendy understood that he wasn't mad at her but that he was upset with his boss and didn't understand why he had made that decision. He decided to go to his boss to find out more.

When he talked to his boss Sam found out that another account that was pending would better use his talents. In fact, Sam had expressed interest in the account last year. Sam agreed that the second account was a better fit than the Fabor account, and was glad that his boss was looking out for him.

Sam worked hard to make sure he didn't fill in the blanks and create a negative drama about the situation. Because he only knew part of the story, Sam possibly could have created a bad situation for himself by creating any of the following negative dramas:

- Wendy got the account because she is a woman, and women are going to get good accounts just because they are women, not because they deserve them.

- Sam is on his way out of the company and this is just a first step in forcing him to leave.

- Sam's abilities are not acknowledged at his company and he'll never move up, so he might as well start looking for another job.

- The boss likes Wendy more than Sam.

Using GPS Thinking in Mental Theater

In a car, a Global Positioning System (GPS) device will alert you when you are going off track and attempt to course correct you to get you to your destination. GPS Beliefs work in a similar manner. GPS Beliefs are those beliefs that are continually course correcting to keep you on track with your GPS Goals—those goals that are identified along the path to your professional destination. We all would benefit from getting out of the habit of our faulty or negative thinking and developing the ability to have GPS Beliefs that get us thinking in the right direction. People in the Smart Zone have GPS Beliefs and GPS Goals.

I discuss GPS Beliefs and GPS Goals in more detail in Part Two of this book, as part of The Smart Zone Life Plan. But I mention GPS thinking here because it's one method you can use to recalculate your mindset when you've filled in the blanks and are trapped in a negative drama. Use the following four questions to recalculate, course correct and get back on track with the right information. These four questions are discussed in more detail in Part Two:

1. Is my thinking based on fact?

2. Does my thinking help me achieve my goal?

3. Does my thinking help me feel the way I want to feel?

4. How can I change my mental theater to create a win-win situation?

By asking yourself these questions, you can course correct your thinking to Work in the Smart Zone and stop yourself from creating a negative drama that can get out of hand.

Triangles are (Unfortunately) Easy to Create

One of the worst things that can happen in Mental Theater is the formation of triangles, which are relationship poison. Triangles are formed when two co-workers have a disagreement, and they involve a third, less powerful person to diffuse the conflict rather than resolving the disagreement between themselves. With this process, called "triangulation," the problem can become bigger than it needs to be.

If you have a problem with a co-worker, talk to the co-worker about it. Although it's difficult, it's part of being in the Smart Zone. If you have a problem with someone, make sure they hear about it from you first. This follows the old saying, "Be loyal to people when they are not present." If you are loyal to them, they are much more likely to do the same with you. Triangles always spell trouble because they prevent the resolution of a conflict between two people. The triangulated person, while possibly trying to be helpful, can be victimized and given part of the responsibility for the problem.

Most professional ethics codes require professionals to talk to a person about a problem first, before talking to other people about it. As a psychologist, if I have concerns about the behavior of another psychologist, the expectation is that I address it with him or her first thing. If a third party needs to be brought in, it is only after exhausting all attempts to address it. This same approach is a good rule of thumb.

You Are in Charge of Your Own Mental Theater

Don't put other people in charge of your mental theater. You are in charge of it. When you start thinking of all the different scenarios that might explain a situation at work, follow these Smart Ideas to create the kind of Mental Theater that keeps you *Working in the Smart Zone*:

- **Say in your head, "Bless his heart."** There are times that someone at work can be offensive or even downright rude. Instead of engaging in the situation, say in your mind "Bless his heart" and you will adjust your reaction so it is more productive and less blaming. This distances you from taking it more personally. You will be better able to move forward and come out the better person.

- **Write out your response before you actually approach someone.** Flesh out your ideas on paper, getting your response straight in your head first. That will help you communicate with that person more effectively.

- **Go back to the source.** Ask for clarification from the source rather than fact finding with others who may contribute to the drama. When you go to the source and give them a chance to fill in the blanks themselves you are better able to manage what you are thinking. Create questions that will help you check out what you need to know. Ask questions like, "I was wondering why Wendy was given that project and I wanted to give you the opportunity to help me understand why I wasn't the best candidate."

- **Use positive affirmations to keep your mind on the right track.** We all hear voices in our heads. Admit it. For most of us the voice doesn't require medication; it's the voice of reason. Make sure that voice is always saying something positive that will keep your thoughts in line and help you benefit the most from Mental Theater. Keep repeating phrases like, "I'm going to keep working hard until I get it right" and "Successful people are willing to do the hard stuff."

Don't Imagine People in Their Underwear

You can use Mental Theater in a positive way by visualizing your success. When you have a big proposal that you have to present, don't visualize yourself doing poorly and being embarrassed. Instead, imagine yourself, step by step, successfully presenting the proposal in front of your audience. Forget the idea of visualizing people in their underwear. Instead, focus on your performance and choreograph yourself giving the presentation.

When you are successful at a task in your own thoughts, you are more likely to be successful when you actually do it. Figure skaters use this approach with their routines, actors do it with their performances, and singers do it for the most important shows. It's the ultimate preparation that will keep you *Working in the Smart Zone.*

SMART Moves

- Address difficult issues instead of trying to overlook them. Ask for clarification from the source rather than fact finding with others who may contribute to the drama. Resist triangulation.

- If you have only part of the story, resist filling in the blanks, as you may end up creating a negative drama that's incorrect. Instead, go back to the source and ask for clarification.

- Use GPS Thinking and GPS Goals to course correct your thoughts and keep yourself from getting trapped in a negative drama.

- Use the creativity of Mental Theater in a positive way to visualize your success. When you are successful at a task in your thoughts, you are more likely to be successful when you actually do it.

Chapter 9

Managing Change

"You mean I don't have a job?"
– Susan Fletcher in 1984

When No Control Brings About Change

Think of one of the most important learning experiences you've ever had. Mine was in 1984 when the job I had been promised at Lee Memorial Hospital in Fort Myers, Florida didn't come through because of budget cuts. I hadn't planned to have to look for another job. I was only 21 at the time but I'm glad I learned the lesson early that life happens when you plan for something else. What I'd expected and planned for fell through, and since I had no control I just had to go with it. That resulted in my moving to Texas where my parents had moved while I was at the University of Florida. Ultimately, it was the best thing that could have happened, even though I didn't see that at the time.

Your learning experience also probably involved an unexpected challenge or change. Think about how it made you stronger and more adaptable. How did you benefit from it?

The Value of Operational Agility

Have you experienced any of these situations?
- Your company was bought out or merged
- Your department was reorganized
- Your boss was promoted or left the company
- You were a victim of downsizing
- Your job description changed
- The weekly staff meeting was moved to a different day
- The coffee pot was moved in the break room

Corporate America has an "adapt or die" mentality. When things change suddenly adaptability is our survival mechanism. In a recent issue of *Fast Company* magazine Charles Fishman says that one of the most important corporate resources over the next 20 years will be operationally agile talent. People will need to be able to thrive on change in order for organizations to remain on the cutting edge.

People in the Smart Zone have enthusiasm for change; they are resilient and innovative. Here are four Smart Ideas for adapting to change in your organization:

- **Take a moment to understand the change in context.** Try to understand the change and its purpose. How will your department benefit from the reorganization? Can communication be improved? Will it help give you an edge over your competitors? Then decide if resisting the change is worth it. Adapting to change is easier when you understand the context of the change.

- **Don't let fear rule.** Fear and anxiety are normal responses to change but they can also impede your ability to adapt. Remain calm in the face of the unexpected. Let your response to a change not be ruled by fear but by your self-confidence.

- **Differentiate yourself.** We all seek change. Think about it— do you like eating lunch at the same restaurant every day, or do you prefer variety? Do you reread the same book every time you get on the airplane, or do you prefer to read a new book every so often? Accept that change is necessary and be the one to give it a try.

- **Stay focused.** Even though everything around you might change, stay focused on the end result of your own job—cutting costs, increasing sales, satisfying customers, managing profit and loss, improving safety—and make decisions that favorably impact the end result of your job.

Adaptability is an Important Secret to Success

It's not enough just to manage change; you have to *drive* change. Adaptability is one key secret to success. Employees who are adaptable add greater value to the organization.

When someone asks me to name the most important skill that we can teach our children, my answer is to manage change; to be adaptable. It's inevitable that your child will face change. We handicap our children if we choreograph their world and deny them the opportunity to manage and ultimately drive change.

In the workplace we have to get along no matter what the change. We can't typically pick the people we work with, the circumstances of our jobs, or the setting. We provide the most value when we are able to adapt to changes that are out of our control and make the best of them. By being adaptable, you are *Working in the Smart Zone.*

Chapter Nine
SMART Moves

- Learning to be adaptable is one of the most important skills you can acquire, because change is inevitable. To deal with it, stay focused on your own job, try to understand why the change is necessary, and don't let fear get in the way.

- Operationally agile employees will be an important corporate resource in the next 20 years. Employees who are agile add value to an organization.

- Teach your children to manage and drive change; it's one of the most important skills to learn. Choreographing their world denies them the opportunity to adapt and learn.

Chapter 10

Managing Mood

"We gain strength, and courage, and confidence by each experience in which we really stop to look fear in the face… we must do that which we think we cannot."
– Eleanor Roosevelt

Optimism and the Yuck Factor

What's the "yuck" you deal with in your job each day? That is, what's the most distasteful and painful thing you face daily? It could be a co-worker, a client, a regular task or a meeting. Starting today, squash the yuck out of your job with an attitude change.

Daniel Goleman calls it the "yuck factor" and Martin E.P. Seligman calls it "hitting the wall." They're referring to the part of your workday when your productivity plummets. You start agonizing over that painful, yucky thing—the next sales call, an upcoming meeting or a task you need to complete. Procrastination sets in. All of a sudden you have given up control of your day and the yucky task is in the driver's seat.

People in the Smart Zone are optimists and know how to overcome the yuck factor before they hit the wall. But before we discuss how to be an optimist let's look at what makes them tick; their personal characteristics and job choices.

Characteristics of an Optimist

Optimists have the following characteristics:

- They are persistent in achieving goals in spite of obstacles and setbacks.
- They feel they can control situations rather than having situations control them.
- They are more popular.
- They are hopeful for success in daily work.
- They have a minimized fear of failure.
- They live longer, healthier lives.

According to Martin E.P. Seligman's book, *Learned Optimism*, if you're in one of these fields then an optimistic outlook is a must:

- sales
- brokering
- public relations
- presenting or acting
- fundraising
- creative jobs
- highly competitive jobs
- high burnout jobs

Some feel that pessimism has its place in Corporate America. Research supports the fact that pessimists have a more accurate take than optimists on some situations because optimists believe they have more control over things than they actually do. If you're an accountant, safety engineer, contract negotiator or technical writer it actually helps to be a little pessimistic.

Improving Optimism

However, optimism is simply more useful in relationships and in life in general. Take the example of a common yuck factor: meeting with a difficult manager. Here are four Smart Ideas for improving optimism in this situation:

- **Take control of the yuck.** Before you reach the yuck factor in your day control it with an attitude you can change or a skill you can acquire. Remind yourself that you're in control of the yuck.

- **Look at the evidence.** Your belief about your manager matters more than the actual meeting itself. The best way to dispute a negative belief is to prove that it's false. Take a quick reality check. Are you sure your manager really wants to yell at you? Are you sure he really dislikes you?

- **Consider other causes.** Most painful or unpleasant events in the world have more than one cause. Pessimists narrow in on one bad cause, which in this case is: "My manager is difficult because he hates me." Optimists realize there are other causes: "My manager is difficult because this organization puts too much pressure on people in management" or "My manager is difficult because he isn't as involved in the daily operations so he doesn't have all of the information. I know what I'm talking about."

- **Keep it real.** So what if you're right? Your manager hates your guts. Is it the end of the world? Just because a meeting doesn't go well doesn't mean life is over. See this as an opportunity to shine by improving next time. Employees who overcome a setback show their value *even more* to their managers and grow personally from the experience.

Contributing to Profitability with Happiness

Creating a world where happiness is a value is catching on. Last year Harvard began teaching students how to be happy in a class called Positive Psychology, and the movie *Happy Feet* won an Academy Award. The king of Bhutan, a small Himalayan kingdom, declared that "gross national happiness is more important than the gross national product." On several fronts our world is finally recognizing that happiness and well-being contributes to profitability and economic growth.

The king of Bhutan recognizes that public policy should be linked to people's sense of well-being and not just to economics, and so does Corporate America. Companies that value the well-being of their employees as much as that of their customers have been shown to actually enjoy higher profits. Jim Collins, author of *Built to Last* and *Good to Great* says that, "Lasting excellence in corporations... stem[s] less from decisions about strategy than decisions about people." Habitually happy people have creative, independent and adventuresome spirits; they appreciate other people, especially those with differences that they can learn from.

People in the Smart Zone are generally optimistic and contribute to a positive work environment. The following are Smart Ideas that any organization can adopt to keep *Working in the Smart Zone*:

- **Use technology to connect people, not to disconnect.**
  According to scientist Alvin Weinberg, "Technology makes it

easier and easier to disconnect from other people, and from ourselves." Remember that human interaction can boost your mood. Make a rule: if an email is more than two paragraphs, pick up the phone and call instead.

- **Finish what you start.** Research shows that being disciplined, deliberate, and finishing projects increases happiness by 18%. It's not always easy to be conscientious and finish a large task, but we feel better about ourselves when we have the sense of accomplishment.

- **Have fun with the "F" word.** Failure, that is. Management guru Tom Peters says each of us should become a "Failure Fanatic." It's like skiing; if you aren't falling down then you aren't learning. Publicly applaud a failure within your organization and reward the process improvement that results from it. Remember failure is feedback.

- **Study happiness.** Tal Ben-Shahar, who teaches the Positive Psychology class at Harvard, says, "You can absolutely teach people how to be happier. While you cannot teach a grouch to be Pollyanna, you can certainly increase people's levels of optimism and happiness." Among the tips offered in his class: Keep it simple, allow yourself to be human, and look at failure as a learning experience.

- **Share a silly moment.** "Laughter may be the shortest distance between two brains," says Daniel Goleman in his book *Social Intelligence*. Think of the immediate sense of closeness you get with someone when you share a nice hearty laugh. In that moment you are in sync with each other's thoughts.

- **Know what makes others happy.** Happy people are attuned to the emotions of others. Try these ideas: Headed to meet with a client? When you grab yourself a latte on the way to the meeting buy one for your client also. Planning to eat lunch out today? Order an extra dessert to bring back for a co-worker. Taking a trip and leaving your co-workers to cover for you? Bring back a small gift from your destination—even just a whimsical trinket from the airport gift shop. When you hear a speaker at a conference, buy his or her book for your assistant or office manager.

- **Smile.** Smile even when you don't feel like it, and you can actually trick your brain's neurotransmitters into thinking you are happy. When you smile at people they typically smile back; it's a natural reflex to mimic the facial expressions of others. If you're in a bad rut, clench a pencil in between your teeth and you'll force your face into a smile. This subtly evokes a positive feeling.

Back in Chapter 7 on Managing Stress we covered a basic truth: the way you think affects the way you act and the way you feel. Learning to manage mood requires adjusting the way you think, the way you feel, and the way you act. By managing your mood and building an environment of optimism and happiness, you can positively contribute to the bottom line. *Working in the Smart Zone* increases profitability and makes your workplace the place where people want to be.

Chapter Ten
SMART Moves

- Change your attitude to help manage the yuck in your day. Remember you're in control. And remember that a setback is not the end of the world. View it as an opportunity to shine next time.

- You can learn to be an optimist. Optimists are persistent in achieving their goals in spite of setbacks, and they feel in control rather than controlled by situations.

- Learning to manage your mood requires adjusting how you think, act and feel.

- Happiness and well-being contribute to profitability and growth. Companies that value the well-being of both their employees and their customers enjoy higher profits. Therefore, building an environment of optimism and change can positively contribute to the bottom line.

Chapter 11

Sanity Sustained

"Go where you feel most like yourself."
– A line from the movie *The Lake House*

There is No Such Thing as Balancing Work and Family Life

I mean it. There is no such thing as balancing your life. Very smart people try and teach us how to have it all, how to be "totally present," and how to be "super" at what we do. The problem is that many people are going crazy trying to do it all. People say to me frequently, "How do you do it all with a business and three kids?" My answer is, "Sometimes not very well but we try our best," and that is really okay with me. See, I believe in trying *not* to balance it all. I believe that you should try and keep your sanity sustained.

Most people think my life is full because I travel to consult with key leaders in companies and I speak at national conferences. While that does make it full, it is really in the month of January that my life feels the most full.

January is the biggest month in our clinical practice. In January a lot of people are attempting to cope with things that occurred during the holidays. New Year's resolutions get people in the mood to work on things about themselves. The beginning of the year for some people is a reminder of what they didn't accomplish the previous year. Every January I go away with my girlfriends for a weekend. Every January I feel the stress of being busy at work and I think I shouldn't go away because I have too much to do. To keep my sanity sustained, I go ahead and go anyway, even though it feels wrong because there are so many things that need my attention.

This past January, on our girls' weekend, we watched the movie, *The Lake House*. It was the line, "Go where you feel most like yourself" that resonated with all of us. I go on these weekends because it helps me feel most like myself. I think everyone should know where they feel most like themselves. It will help keep your sanity sustained.

The Sleep Test

There's a simple test that helps you know if you're doing it right. It's called the Sleep Test. Do you go to bed at night able to sleep because you've been productive? Or do you have too much unfinished business that keeps you up at night? The answer to keeping your sanity sustained isn't a prescription for Ambien or another sleep medication. The question really is, "Do you make it right with yourself?" Keeping your sanity sustained involves integrity, responsibility, and managing your energy and attention. All of these are important to *Working in the Smart Zone*.

Living a Life of Integrity

Integrity is sticking to your code of conduct. It's basing your actions on an internally consistent framework of principles. You have integrity when everything you do and believe is based on the same core set of values. Integrity is linked to responsibility and accountability. People with integrity hold themselves accountable and manage their responsibilities.

Here are the benefits of living with Integrity:

1. **You are respected.** People respect you and are more likely to follow you because you act more honestly.

2. **You have fewer regrets.** When you follow your own code of ethics, you know the difference between right and wrong and you don't regret anything you've done.

3. **You are less likely to be sued, fired, or dumped.**

4. **You are better able to speak on your own behalf, not needing others to speak for you.**

5. **You tell the truth.** You don't have to worry about keeping stories straight because you tell the truth consistently and accurately.

6. **You can manage your response to criticism.** People who have integrity act fairly.

7. **People want to know you and work with you.** It's more emotionally comfortable for people to be around someone with integrity.

8. **You like yourself and are liked by other people.**

9. **The world is a place of opportunity rather than regret.**

10. **You don't have to waste energy trying to hide mistakes from others.** When you make mistakes you are better able to hold yourself accountable and take responsibility.

Living a Life of Responsibility

Being responsible means being able to be counted on. When you are responsible to yourself, to other people, and to the role you play in your organization, you are more likely to succeed. People who are not responsible are eliminated, transferred, not chosen, and possibly demoted.

Here are the benefits of living with Responsibility:

1. **You are given more opportunities.** People who are responsible are seen as successful.

2. **You are less likely to be micromanaged.**

3. **You will be favored for higher positions and promotions.** Responsible people are more likely to complete tasks so they are typically on the list for promotions.

4. **You immerse yourself in tasks at an appropriate level.** You are less likely to accept responsibility when you are not likely to succeed.

5. **You are more likely to be recognized.** Others will know when you manage responsibilities because you are seen as a leader rather than a follower.

6. **You will be seen as a go-to person.** Co-workers will know that you know what you're doing and manage your tasks well.

7. **You are better able to turn down responsibility.** This is because others see you as a "doer" rather than as someone who just does enough to get by. You are more likely to be given a free pass when it's appropriate.

8. **You can be trusted with trade secrets and intellectual property.** You have proven that you are not likely to be sloppy with information.

9. **You get noticed.** You have higher visibility as a person who is responsible.

10. **Your word is trusted.**

Living a Life of Managing Energy and Attention

At the beginning of this book, we pointed out that time management is for rookies. Being in the Smart Zone is not about time management. The folks who believe in balancing work and family life would talk to you about time management. Instead, the Smart Zone strategy of sanity sustained promotes managing energy and attention.

Here are the benefits of Managing Energy and Attention:

1. **You get to decide the tasks that make sense to you.** You are less likely to be overcommitted because you get to decide what gives you energy and what drains you. Choosing to be involved in those things that give you energy keeps your sanity sustained.

2. **You evaluate technology.** The latest technological gadgets do not always make your life easier. In fact, sometimes life gets more difficult with a BlackBerry or a voice-activated computer program. Deciding if now is the time that you want to devote your energy and attention helps you manage yourself better, rather than deciding based on having a free afternoon to figure it out.

3. **You're allowed to take mental vacations.** White space in your head is so important in the day. Taking a few minutes to switch the attention in your brain can actually increase productivity. Sitting at a computer for more than 20 minutes without a break actually contributes to decreased productivity because the intensity of your focus can be compromised. More frequent breaks help you manage your attention and energy and keep you on task.

4. **When you manage your attention and energy, you keep reserves for when it's most important.** You manage your thoughts and activity level so you're giving your best when it matters.

5. **You sleep better.** At the end of the evening you're less likely to be exhausted because you know how to stop yourself from being totally spent.

6. **Your family is less likely to get the worst of you.** Even though I believe that marriage brings out the worst in us because we say things to our spouses that we'd never say to co-workers, we need to be better about being at our best in our family relationships. When you manage your attention and energy, you're less likely to go home resentful that you've had little time to yourself.

7. **You keep your social relationships.** By being aware of when you need a break and when you need some time with friends, you're less likely to let too much time slip by before reconnecting with the friendships that matter.

8. **You stay well rounded.** A one-dimensional person is boring. When you keep your interests and have something new to contribute, people are more likely to be interested in you and want to get to know you. If you haven't read a newspaper in weeks, you're going to be out in left field during some conversations.

9. **You're less likely to be late or to miss deadlines.** Because you're aware of what's on your plate, you can be counted on.

10. **You age more slowly.** The stress of being out of sync and not being in charge of your life increases the stress hormones that contribute to aging. By managing your attention and energy you are better able to self preserve, both internally and externally.

Trying to balance work and family life can make you crazy. Instead, work for sanity sustained. Live with integrity, responsibility, and by managing your attention and energy. You'll be more likely to be able to do it all by your standards and to continue *Working in the Smart Zone*.

Chapter Eleven
SMART Moves

- If you live a life of integrity, you'll never have to worry about keeping your story straight, and you won't regret anything you've done. People will want to be around you, they'll like you, and you'll like yourself.

- If you live a life of responsibility, you'll have more opportunities, you'll get noticed, and you're more likely to be promoted and be successful. People who are not responsible are eliminated, transferred, not chosen, and possibly demoted.

- If you live your life by managing your energy and attention, you'll get to decide on the tasks that make sense to you. As a result you'll stay well rounded, you'll be less likely to be late or miss deadlines, and you'll sleep better and age less slowly.

Chapter 12

Likeability

"We judges ourselves by our intentions
and others by their behavior."
– Stephen M. R. Covey

The Real Reason People Leave Organizations

William Heyman, CEO of Heyman Associates, a leading executive search firm, studied the essence of leadership success over a three-year period. He found that a leader's success is measured in part by how well he or she gets along with others. This is consistent with what we already know. People don't leave organizations; people leave their bosses.

Leadership vs. Social Competency

Since we know that people leave people, not jobs, it's not enough to know just about leadership. It would benefit all of us to know about social competency, the ability to achieve personal goals in social interaction while simultaneously maintaining positive relationships with others, over time and across situations.

According to Hara Estroff Marano, Editor of *Psychology Today*, several elements are involved in the healthy development of social competency:

- sociable disposition
- pro-social orientation (the root of empathy)
- emotion regulation
- reading emotional states
- initiating interaction
- group or game entry
- responsiveness
- paying attention to relationships
- handling provocation
- managing disagreements without fighting

According to Tim Sanders, the author of *The Likeability Factor*, "Likeability is the ability to create positive attitudes in other people through the delivery of functional and psychological benefits." There is no doubt that likeability is a key component in leadership success. Sanders teaches us that, "Organizations have traditionally focused on the competencies and thinking ability of their staff. There is growing recognition, however, that job effectiveness can be undone if an employee is not likeable."

It is a detriment to a company when unlikeable people are doing business. Not surprisingly, likeability is also a factor in getting elected to public office. Gallup's personality factor poll, conducted prior to every presidential election since 1960, has found that likeability is one of only three factors, the others being issues and party affiliation, that has been a consistent predictor of the final election result.

When Someone is Unlikeable

For children as well as adults, nothing predicts being disliked more than aggression and negative interactions. And those negative interactions can begin a cycle that's difficult to break. According to the experts, difficult or unlikeable people are most often dismissed or ignored, meaning that unlikeable people may experience a high degree of emotional loneliness, and over time can become more and more socially isolated. Isolation in turn can create distorted ways of thinking.

Some characteristics that make someone not likeable include:
- trying too hard
- being unfocused
- having a poor code of ethics
- being unable to control insecurities
- not being a team player
- providing little value at work
- seeming judgmental
- exhibiting a negative attitude
- appearing self-centered
- seeming too busy to notice you
- acting in a disrespectful way to others
- taking credit for others' ideas
- being a know-it-all
- being untrustworthy

The Four Factors of Likeability

According to *The Likeability Factor* by Tim Sanders, the four critical elements of your personality that will help raise your Likeability Factor are:

1. **Friendliness:** your ability to communicate liking and openness to others.

2. **Relevance:** your capacity to connect with others' interests, wants, and needs.

3. **Empathy:** your ability to recognize, acknowledge, and experience other people's feelings.

4. **Realness:** the integrity that stands behind your likeability and guarantees its authenticity.

Adding to Likeability

Other factors that make people more likeable:

- **Dressing in a similar manner.** You'll relate better to someone who is dressed in a similar way to you, whether that's a matter of being formal or informal, or having a similar style or taste. Similarity builds trust.

- **Being physically attractive.** Social psychology shows that attractive people tend to draw attention and are judged to be smarter, kinder, more honest, and more approachable.

- **Using a pleasant tone of voice.** If you smile while you're talking, even when leaving a voicemail, people are more likely to remember you, listen to you and respond to you.

- **Having the power to help you advance.** Your likeability increases when you are perceived to be able to help someone.

- **Engaging in a pleasant activity.** You are more likely to close a deal when you are having lunch with someone. Your proposal is better received when you are doing something that is enjoyable, without pressure, and where you are having a good time.

If you feel you deserve a promotion but can't figure out why it's not happening, ask yourself if you're likeable. Likeability is a key factor in determining success at all levels. Many people make the mistake of assuming that just because they like themselves, other people like them too. That is not a guarantee. Likeability is based on solid principles that can be followed and developed. You can improve your likeability factor, which can in turn lead not only to *Working in the Smart Zone* but also to finding success by becoming a leader others want to follow.

Chapter Twelve
SMART Moves

- Likeability is important in a work setting, and in predicting success at all levels. In fact, it's a detriment to a company to have an unlikeable person doing business on its behalf. There's also growing evidence that a person's job effectiveness can be undone if that person is not likeable.

- Not surprisingly, likeability is crucial in getting elected to public office, but it's necessary for all leaders. In fact, a leader's success is measured in part by how well he or she gets along with others.

- Likeability is based on solid principles. You can improve your likeability factor by exhibiting friendliness, relevance, empathy and realness. By being more likeable you increase your chances of becoming a leader others want to follow.

Chapter 13

The Smart Zone Secret

*"What you take is how you make a living.
What you give is how you make your life."*
– Winston Churchill

Take the Focus Off of Yourself

The Smart Zone Secret is critical for reducing stress, resolving conflicts and improving productivity. Many of you who have participated in my workshops and have seen my presentations know that I frequently end the event by revealing the Smart Zone Secret: Take the focus off of yourself.

By becoming outwardly focused on others we can generate positive energy and create an atmosphere of collaboration and encouragement. Both individuals and organizations can benefit from the Smart Zone Secret.

Here are four Smart Ideas you and your organization can use to take the focus off yourself:

1. **Get involved in something bigger than yourself.** For example, learn about the 3R's: Reduce, Reuse, Recycle. Even Wal-Mart sells organic cotton t-shirts these days, and it was recently reported that Southfork Ranch (of TV series *Dallas* fame) near my home had "gone green." I know EPA and OSHA concerns are paramount in many of today's work environments, but take a moment to investigate the small ways you can help: recycling, carpooling, turning your thermostat up (or down) by a few degrees, donating your magazines and catalogues to hospitals or schools, reusing shopping bags, and educating your children on environmental issues.

2. **Volunteer your time.** One sure way to take the focus off yourself is to experience the joy of helping others. To find a place to volunteer check with your Human Resources department or with volunteer agencies in your community. At www.VolunteerMatch.org you can type in your ZIP code and find hundreds of places looking for volunteers. I typed in my ZIP code and found 453 opportunities!

3. **Toughen up.** One trait that leaders possess is resilience, tough mindedness and the ability to accept criticism. A recent study

by PsyMax Solutions of more than 2,000 employees' profiles revealed that middle managers had the highest median score on tough-mindedness while CEOs had the lowest. The firm suggested this could be because middle managers typically deal with day-to-day operations and must accept input from all directions within the organization. To be more resilient you must be willing to speak openly and be a little vulnerable.

4. **Connect with people.** The most important way to take the focus off of yourself is to reach out and connect with people you meet. Find out the name of the janitor at your company, say hello to the toll booth worker as he takes your change, ask your waiter how she is doing today, talk to someone in the elevator, give a genuine compliment to a co-worker... You get the message!

Extend the Smart Zone Secret

If you haven't seen the movie, *Pay It Forward*, you need to rent it. Put it in your Netflix Queue. It came out in 2000, a year before we all dealt with the World Trade Center falling down on 9/11. The message is clear: extend good deeds. The Smart Zone Secret also challenges you to extend the Smart Zone Secret. Here are some Smart Ideas to get you started:

- Engage in a short unscripted conversation when people least expect it.

- Look people in the eye and smile warmly as they talk to you. Let them set the pace of the conversation and work hard to resist one-upping them or making the conversation about you.

- Create a positive experience for other people and you'll create one for yourself too.

- You don't need to get deep in conversation with people to make a difference. Sometimes we are more effective when we don't know the content of their stress.

- Don't make people compete for your attention. Put the cell phone down, take your hand off the door handle, and don't check email when you are on a conference call.

- Tell people you appreciate them. Say "Please" and "Thank you" even when you think it's not necessary. These small gestures go a long way to create a Smart Zone Environment.

The Importance of the Smart Zone Secret

You know the restaurant you'll be eating at tonight? What you don't know is that the server worked a double last night, the third one this week to make more money. Because it rained last night, the restaurant wasn't busy and he was short on tips. This morning he woke up very discouraged because he doesn't have the cash to register for college courses this semester. He can't get loans and he has no one in his life that can help him out financially. He's trying to decide if he should just not go to school this semester and work instead to save money so he can pay his rent and maybe go back to school next semester. We can all appreciate how hard it would be to return once he's sat out a semester. He's afraid he won't finish school.

You know your dry cleaner? While she always has a smile on her face, she's facing what may be the most difficult decision in her life. Her mother has lived with her for eight years, but it's becoming increasingly hard to care for her since she developed Alzheimer's two years ago. Last night, her mother left the house in the middle of the night thinking she needed to walk home from school. Her memory had failed her, and she thought she was 13 years old spending the night at a friend's house when actually, she's 87 and very fragile. The dry cleaner fears she'll fall and get hurt or leave the house and get lost. She's having difficulty caring for her mother since she also has a husband, a business, and three small children. She always promised herself she'd take care of her mother, so it's tearing her apart to realize her mother needs to be in an assisted living facility. She's tormented by guilt and feeling very hopeless.

Then there's the toll booth operator on the toll road that you take to work. Most people have TollTags and those who don't just throw in coins or get their change from the toll booth operator without saying a word. Most people don't even acknowledge that a person is in the booth. They're so busy with their own lives that they just focus on getting on their way as fast as they can. Today is a different day for the tollbooth

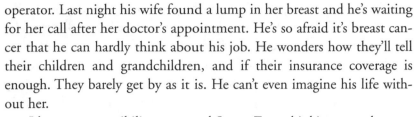

operator. Last night his wife found a lump in her breast and he's waiting for her call after her doctor's appointment. He's so afraid it's breast cancer that he can hardly think about his job. He wonders how they'll tell their children and grandchildren, and if their insurance coverage is enough. They barely get by as it is. He can't even imagine his life without her.

It's your responsibility to extend Smart Zone thinking now that you know the Smart Zone Secret. By taking the focus off of yourself you can put the focus on other people without even knowing their lives. You don't have to know about the server's school predicament, the dry cleaner's guilt about her mother, or the toll booth operator's fears about his wife's possible diagnosis. You can make a difference in their lives by engaging with them and presenting an image of optimism and happiness, and by using your skills of Emotional Intelligence you can move them towards being in the Smart Zone.

You know the server you'll see at the restaurant tonight? When he starts to tell you the specials, wait for him to finish, make eye contact and ask him what he likes best on the menu. If you engage in conversation and make it an enjoyable evening for him and for you, you can help him enhance his mood where his thinking will be more solution oriented. You could create an environment where he becomes more hopeful and decides to talk to someone at the university to see if there's a payment plan, because he can't imagine himself not taking classes.

Then there's the dry cleaner. We all understand the dilemmas of the sandwich generation, who have to care for their parents as well as their own children who still live at home. As she worries about her mother and what to do, you walk in to pick up your suits. You've always noticed the fresh flowers on the counter. This time, say something about them. Show interest in the fact that she goes the extra mile to make her store inviting and lively. Listen to her, look her in the eye, and smile when she talks about how she likes to go pick them out herself. Show the interest and the four likeability factors that will also make her feel more likeable. It won't help her solve the situation with her mother any faster but it will help her feel more competent and confident about the difficult decision that she faces. By having you engage and show interest, she is likely to feel significant and capable. You can help her feel more hopeful in her day, which will also help her keep her sanity sustained as she focuses a lot of attention on her difficult decision.

Finally, there's the tollbooth operator. Even just a 10-second interaction, like saying good morning and acknowledging his presence, can help him snap out of the worry that he feels for his wife's medical crisis. Because worry is the misuse of imagination, it's likely that your brief interaction will stop him from imagining the worst. You can't improve his situation but you can help him stabilize himself. Through just a short interaction, you can make a difference by helping him think more optimistically as his wife's medical situation unfolds. Extending the Smart Zone Secret to him is likely to help him stay strong *Working in the Smart Zone* as he supports her.

SMART Moves

- The Smart Zone Secret is simple: take the focus off of yourself. It'll help you reduce stress, resolve conflicts and improve productivity.

- By living the Smart Zone Secret you'll create positive energy and a generous, collaborative atmosphere, and you'll end up creating a positive experience for yourself too. Try getting involved in a cause or volunteering your time, and most important, make sure you're connecting with other people.

- Extend Smart Zone thinking to others. You can do this in many small ways that have a big impact. Start up a conversation, tell someone you appreciate him, look someone in the eye when you're talking to her, and say please and thank you. Small gestures go a long way in creating a Smart Zone Environment.

PART TWO

The Smart Zone
Life Plan

Chapter 14

*What is a Smart Zone
Life Plan?*

Now that you are reading about *Working in the Smart Zone*, it is clear that you have the desire to improve your current business and/or personal situation. Careers are more successful when there is a plan. But don't let someone else's plan for you drive the bus—you need to be in the driver's seat, and a Smart Zone Life Plan will put you there. With a Smart Zone Life Plan, your butt will be better planted to see the road you have set for yourself, even when there are unavoidable pit stops.

The Steps in the Life Plan

Although the process of developing a Smart Zone Life Plan is straightforward, it is not something you can do in one sitting. In the beginning it is a big-time work in progress. Others who've done it describe it as a homework assignment that's bigger than they expected.

The ugly side of a Life Plan is that it is always a work in progress. But the beauty of a Life Plan is that it is always a work in progress. Just like a business plan, it should continually be consulted and revised in some areas while the basic vision stays pretty much on course. That is why I talk about your GPS Beliefs (introduced in Chapter 8: Mental Theater) that are part of building the competencies to be a business person in the Smart Zone and building the competencies to live a Smart Zone Lifestyle.

GPS Beliefs are part of moving forward instead of looking back. GPS Beliefs work very much like a Global Positioning System. GPS Beliefs get you to your destination by course correcting when you get off track. You want to have GPS Beliefs because they are what keep you in the Smart Zone. Identifying your GPS Beliefs is a major component of the Life Plan.

The Life Plan is based on developing specific competencies: the *6 Competencies of a Business Person in the Smart Zone* (Chapter 16) and the *8 Competencies of a Smart Zone Lifestyle* (Chapter 17). We'll discuss each of the 14 competencies separately, which will help you to identify where you have faulty thinking (Looking Back) or where you have GPS Beliefs (Moving Forward).

In this chapter we will use a midlevel manager named Jack as an example. Jack wants to move up and grow professionally in his company. He is just beginning to develop his Life Plan and his examples will help you learn more about how to do your own.

To complete your Life Plan you will follow 3 steps, which are further explained in this chapter:

Step One: Decide which competency you want to work on

Step Two: Complete the Looking Back Worksheet for that competency, using your own personal data
- Current Life Mode
- GPS Goals
- Wisdom You Have Gained

Step Three: Complete the Moving Forward Worksheet for that competency, using your own personal data
- Smart Zone Thinking
- Accountability Mechanism
- Steps to Success

Step One: Decide Which Competency You Want to Work on

The Smart Zone Life Plan is based on the following competencies:

6 Competencies for a Business Person in the Smart Zone
1. Business Management
2. Skill Management
3. Relationship Management
4. Knowledge Management
5. Mentor Management
6. Daily Management

8 Competencies for a Smart Zone Lifestyle
1. Self-Management
2. Health Management

3. Relationship Management

4. Fitness Management

5. Skill Management

6. Emotion Management

7. Financial Management

8. Daily Management

These competencies represent areas of your business or your life where you need to take inventory. They are explained in Chapter 16: *6 Competencies for a Business Person in the Smart Zone* and in Chapter 17: *8 Competencies for a Smart Zone Lifestyle*. Jack decided to work on the Business Management Competency first.

Step Two: Complete the Looking Back Worksheet For That Competency, Using Your Own Personal Data

First you will fill out the Looking Back worksheet, using your own personal data to capture your *Old/Negative/Irrational Beliefs*. On the same worksheet you will capture the *Experiences or Contributing Factors* for those beliefs.

Here is Jack's example:

Business Management—Looking Back Smart Zone Business Competency	
Old/Negative/Inappropriate Beliefs That Keep You Out of Your Smart Zone	**Experiences/ Contributing Factors**
Without a Masters in Business, there is no way that I will get a promotion and be in a Management position.	1. The most recent promotion was given to a guy with an MBA. 2. I have been with the company longer than others who have already been promoted. 3. My immediate supervisor has never brought up the possibility of my being in a management position during my reviews.

Jack: Midlevel Manager wanting to be promoted

Identify Your Current Life Mode:
(The one you want to change/tells about the way you think)

Identify Your GPS Goals:

Identify the Wisdom You Have Gained:

Identify Your Current Life Mode (Looking Back)

Identifying your current life mode that is reinforced by your *Old/Negative/Irrational Beliefs* helps you identify how the irrational beliefs are keeping you out of your Smart Zone. This life mode should be one that you want to change and it tells more about the way you think. Using Jack's example above, his Current Life Mode can be described as the following:

> I am in a "No Win" situation in my job unless I prove my ability to learn how to manage and supervise others. It is important for me to show my leadership abilities and be able to compete with the "big boys" who have their MBA's.

Identify Your GPS Goals (Looking Back)

At this point, you have identified the components of:

- Looking Back (*Old/Negative/Irrational Beliefs* and the *Experiences or Contributing Factors for those Beliefs*)
- Identifying Your Current Life Mode

Now it is time to Identify Your GPS Goals, which you will consider later as you work on the Moving Forward Worksheet. GPS Goals are those goals that you are working towards using the Smart Zone Strategies, Smart Zone Thinking and your GPS Beliefs (*New/Current Beliefs*). The GPS Goals keep the GPS Beliefs in a mode of course correction so you stay on track.

Considering Jack's example, a few of his GPS Goals included the following:

> 1. Be considered for a management position at my company in the next year.
>
> 2. Tell my immediate supervisor that I want to be considered for a management position.
>
> 3. Be qualified for a management position based on my skills and experience.

4. Continue to gain experience that will allow me to develop skills important in a management position.

5. Take on extra responsibility at work so my management skills are visible.

6. Ask for what I want at work.

Identify the Wisdom You Have Gained (Looking Back)

This is simple. All life experiences have the opportunity to help us develop wisdom. The best definition I have found for wisdom is from Wikipedia:

> *Wisdom is a trait that can be developed by experience, but not taught. It may be possessed independent of experience or complete knowledge. It is often looked at as his/her ideals and principles that govern all actions and decisions. Applications of personal wisdom include the ethical and social guidelines that determine the nature of short- and long-term goals pursued in life.*

Record the wisdom you have gained.

The wisdom Jack has gained includes the following:

I am not pleased with the fact that I have not gotten a promotion yet and I realize now that I haven't tried hard enough. You have to ask for what you want and it is possible that my supervisor isn't even aware of my goals in this company. It is up to me to make this happen and I realize now that I have been waiting for someone to hand it to me.

Step Three: Complete the Moving Forward Worksheet For That Competency, Using Your Own Personal Data

Next you will be filling out the Moving Forward worksheet for the same competency, using more of your personal data.

In Moving Forward you will identify your GPS Beliefs that are your *New/Current Beliefs* that will help you Work in the Smart Zone. These beliefs will relate to the *6 Competencies for a Business Person in the Smart Zone* and the *8 Competencies for a Smart Zone Lifestyle*. Reinforcing the GPS Beliefs are the *Observations and Supporting Factors to Reinforce the Beliefs*.

Here is an example from Jack:

Business Management—Moving Forward Smart Zone Business Competency	
GPS Beliefs: Current/New Beliefs That Will Keep You in Your Smart Zone	**Observations/Supporting Factors to Reinforce Beliefs**
Even without a Masters in Business, I am management material. I am committed to learning as much as I can to earn the opportunity for a promotion to management.	1. I participate in more training than is required for my current position. 2. I have been involved in a mentor relationship with one of the most successful and most well respected managers in the company. 3. Others seek my advice & guidance. 4. I save the company money.

Jack: Midlevel Manager wanting to be promoted

Build Your Smart Zone Life Mode:
(The one you want to have/your new way of thinking)

Identify Your Accountability Mechanisms:

Identify Your Steps to Success:

Build Your Smart Zone Life Mode (Moving Forward)

Identifying your Smart Zone thinking comes from your GPS Beliefs and builds your Smart Zone Life Mode. These are your healthier *Current/New Beliefs* that will keep you in your Smart Zone. For Jack, his GPS Belief is:

> *Even without a Masters in Business, I am management material. I am committed to learning as much as I can to earn the opportunity for a promotion to management.*

With this way of thinking, he is course correcting his ability to move in the right direction, believing in his ability. This will guide him towards his GPS Goals, much in the same way a GPS guides you in the right direction. When you get off track (such as with faulty beliefs), you can course correct yourself to move in the right direction. The right direction is what you accomplish with Smart Zone thinking.

Identify Your Accountability Mechanisms (Moving Forward)

Accountability Mechanisms are people or systems you have put in place to catch you when you deviate from your Smart Zone Life Plan. Accountability Mechanisms are explained more fully in Chapter 19. Developing Accountability Mechanisms is a way to build self-trust and to use the trust you have in others to hold you to the goal. Examples of Accountability Mechanisms Jack can develop include:

> 1. *I will tell my closest friend that I plan to participate in additional training to further develop my management skills. I will ask him to follow up with me and hold me accountable to be involved.*
>
> 2. *I will ask my immediate supervisor to set goals with me to help me grow in my position. We will review those goals quarterly to make sure I am on track and moving in the right direction with developing my skills and my experience.*

Identify Your Steps to Success (Moving Forward)

Finally, you will outline the Steps to Success that will continue to keep you moving forward to build the competencies of a Business Person in the Smart Zone and to live a Smart Zone Lifestyle. While it may seem that there is some repetition, it is important to be specific and use action words in each step. If possible, set deadlines to complete each step.

Here are the specific steps to success that Jack wrote down:

1. I will talk with my supervisor at my next review and ask him to sit down with me quarterly to outline ways that I can develop my skills and experience to be more valuable to our company.

2. I will sign up for one business course that will expand my skills next semester.

3. I will set 10 specific goals with my mentor that will help me benefit the most from that relationship.

By following these steps you will move forward with your Smart Zone Life Plan. This is a work in progress and we encourage you to keep it with you so you can identify what you need to do to make progress and to manage the plan you set. By doing so you will be *Working in Your Smart Zone.*

Summary of Smart Zone Competencies

Here is a table that summarizes the Smart Zone Competencies. You'll see that some are included in both the Lifestyle and Business Competencies.

	Lifestyle Competency	Business Competency
Business Management (BM)		X
Relationship Management (RM)	X	X
Knowledge Management (KM)		X
Mentor Management (MM)		X
Self-Management (SfM)	X	
Health Management (HM)	X	
Fitness Management (FtM)	X	
Skill Management (SkM)	X	X
Emotion Management (EM)	X	
Financial Management (FnM)	X	
Daily Management (DM)	X	X

For each competency you decide to work on, you will fill out two worksheets, which are included in Chapter 15. If you'd like additional worksheets, email me at Susan@SmartZoneExpert.com. Put in the subject line: "Life Plan Worksheets" and we'll be happy to send you the Word documents.

Chapter 15

*Smart Zone Life Plan
Original Worksheets:
Looking Back
Moving Forward*

Business Management – Looking Back
Smart Zone Business Competency

Old/Negative/Inappropriate Beliefs That Keep You Out of Your Smart Zone	Experiences/Contributing Factors
1.	1.
2.	2.
3.	3.
4.	4.
5.	5.

Identify Your Current Life Mode:
(The one you want to change/tells about the way you think)

Identify Your GPS Goals:
1.
2.
3.
4.
5.

Identify the Wisdom You Have Gained:

Business Management – Moving Forward
Smart Zone Business Competency

GPS Beliefs: Current/New Beliefs That Will Keep You in Your Smart Zone	Observations/Supporting Factors to Reinforce Beliefs
1.	1.
2.	2.
3.	3.
4.	4.
5.	5.

Build Your Smart Zone Life Mode:
(The one you want to have/your new way of thinking)

Identify Your Accountability Mechanisms:
1.
2.
3.
4.
5.

Identify Your Steps to Success:

Relationship Management – Looking Back
Smart Zone Business Competency

Old/Negative/Inappropriate Beliefs That Keep You Out of Your Smart Zone	Experiences/Contributing Factors
1.	1.
2.	2.
3.	3.
4.	4.
5.	5.

Identify Your Current Life Mode:
(The one you want to change/tells about the way you think)

Identify Your GPS Goals:
1.
2.
3.
4.
5.

Identify the Wisdom You Have Gained:

Relationship Management — Moving Forward
Smart Zone Business Competency

GPS Beliefs: Current/New Beliefs That Will Keep You in Your Smart Zone	Observations/Supporting Factors to Reinforce Beliefs
I.	I.
2.	2.
3.	3.
4.	4.
5.	5.

Build Your Smart Zone Life Mode:
(The one you want to have/your new way of thinking)

Identify Your Accountability Mechanisms:
1.
2.
3.
4.
5.

Identify Your Steps to Success:

Knowledge Management – Looking Back
Smart Zone Business Competency

Old/Negative/Inappropriate Beliefs That Keep You Out of Your Smart Zone	Experiences/Contributing Factors
1.	1.
2.	2.
3.	3.
4.	4.
5.	5.

Identify Your Current Life Mode:
(The one you want to change/tells about the way you think)

Identify Your GPS Goals:
1.
2.
3.
4.
5.

Identify the Wisdom You Have Gained:

Knowledge Management — Moving Forward
Smart Zone Business Competency

GPS Beliefs: Current/New Beliefs That Will Keep You in Your Smart Zone	Observations/Supporting Factors to Reinforce Beliefs
1.	1.
2.	2.
3.	3.
4.	4.
5.	5.

Build Your Smart Zone Life Mode:
(The one you want to have/your new way of thinking)

Identify Your Accountability Mechanisms:
1.
2.
3.
4.
5.

Identify Your Steps to Success:

Mentor Management – Looking Back
Smart Zone Business Competency

Old/Negative/Inappropriate Beliefs That Keep You Out of Your Smart Zone	Experiences/Contributing Factors
1.	1.
2.	2.
3.	3.
4.	4.
5.	5.

Identify Your Current Life Mode:
(The one you want to change/tells about the way you think)

Identify Your GPS Goals:
1.
2.
3.
4.
5.

Identify the Wisdom You Have Gained:

Mentor Management – Moving Forward
Smart Zone Business Competency

GPS Beliefs: Current/New Beliefs That Will Keep You in Your Smart Zone	Observations/Supporting Factors to Reinforce Beliefs
1.	1.
2.	2.
3.	3.
4.	4.
5.	5.

Build Your Smart Zone Life Mode:
(The one you want to have/your new way of thinking)

Identify Your Accountability Mechanisms:
1.
2.
3.
4.
5.

Identify Your Steps to Success:

Skill Management – Looking Back
Smart Zone Business Competency

Old/Negative/Inappropriate Beliefs That Keep You Out of Your Smart Zone	Experiences/Contributing Factors
1.	1.
2.	2.
3.	3.
4.	4.
5.	5.

Identify Your Current Life Mode:
(The one you want to change/tells about the way you think)

Identify Your GPS Goals:
1.
2.
3.
4.
5.

Identify the Wisdom You Have Gained:

Skill Management – Moving Forward
Smart Zone Business Competency

GPS Beliefs: Current/New Beliefs That Will Keep You in Your Smart Zone	Observations/Supporting Factors to Reinforce Beliefs
1.	1.
2.	2.
3.	3.
4.	4.
5.	5.

Build Your Smart Zone Life Mode:
(The one you want to have/your new way of thinking)

Identify Your Accountability Mechanisms:
1.
2.
3.
4.
5.

Identify Your Steps to Success:

Daily Management – Looking Back
Smart Zone Business Competency

Old/Negative/Inappropriate Beliefs That Keep You Out of Your Smart Zone	Experiences/Contributing Factors
1.	1.
2.	2.
3.	3.
4.	4.
5.	5.

Identify Your Current Life Mode:
(The one you want to change/tells about the way you think)

Identify Your GPS Goals:
1.
2.
3.
4.
5.

Identify the Wisdom You Have Gained:

Daily Management — Moving Forward
Smart Zone Business Competency

GPS Beliefs: Current/New Beliefs That Will Keep You in Your Smart Zone	Observations/Supporting Factors to Reinforce Beliefs
1.	1.
2.	2.
3.	3.
4.	4.
5.	5.

Build Your Smart Zone Life Mode:
(The one you want to have/your new way of thinking)

Identify Your Accountability Mechanisms:
1.
2.
3.
4.
5.

Identify Your Steps to Success:

Relationship Management – Looking Back
Smart Zone Lifestyle Competency

Old/Negative/Inappropriate Beliefs That Keep You Out of Your Smart Zone	Experiences/Contributing Factors
1.	1.
2.	2.
3.	3.
4.	4.
5.	5.

Identify Your Current Life Mode:
(The one you want to change/tells about the way you think)

Identify Your GPS Goals:
1.
2.
3.
4.
5.

Identify the Wisdom You Have Gained:

Relationship Management – Moving Forward
Smart Zone Lifestyle Competency

GPS Beliefs: Current/New Beliefs That Will Keep You in Your Smart Zone	Observations/Supporting Factors to Reinforce Beliefs
1.	1.
2.	2.
3.	3,
4.	4.
5.	5.

Build Your Smart Zone Life Mode:
(The one you want to have/your new way of thinking)

Identify Your Accountability Mechanisms:
1.
2.
3.
4.
5.

Identify Your Steps to Success:

Self-Management — Looking Back
Smart Zone Lifestyle Competency

Old/Negative/Inappropriate Beliefs That Keep You Out of Your Smart Zone	Experiences/Contributing Factors
1.	1.
2.	2.
3.	3.
4.	4.
5.	5.

Identify Your Current Life Mode:
(The one you want to change/tells about the way you think)

Identify Your GPS Goals:
1.
2.
3.
4.
5.

Identify the Wisdom You Have Gained:

Self-Management – Moving Forward
Smart Zone Lifestyle Competency

GPS Beliefs: Current/New Beliefs That Will Keep You in Your Smart Zone	Observations/Supporting Factors to Reinforce Beliefs
1.	1.
2.	2.
3.	3.
4.	4.
5.	5.

Build Your Smart Zone Life Mode:
(The one you want to have/your new way of thinking)

Identify Your Accountability Mechanisms:
1.
2.
3.
4.
5.

Identify Your Steps to Success:

Health Management – Looking Back
Smart Zone Lifestyle Competency

Old/Negative/Inappropriate Beliefs That Keep You Out of Your Smart Zone	Experiences/Contributing Factors
1.	1.
2.	2.
3.	3.
4.	4.
5.	5.

Identify Your Current Life Mode:
(The one you want to change/tells about the way you think)

Identify Your GPS Goals:
1.
2.
3.
4.
5.

Identify the Wisdom You Have Gained:

Health Management — Moving Forward
Smart Zone Lifestyle Competency

GPS Beliefs: Current/New Beliefs That Will Keep You in Your Smart Zone	Observations/Supporting Factors to Reinforce Beliefs
1.	1.
2.	2.
3.	3.
4.	4.
5.	5.

Build Your Smart Zone Life Mode:
(The one you want to have/your new way of thinking)

Identify Your Accountability Mechanisms:
1.
2.
3.
4.
5.

Identify Your Steps to Success:

Fitness Management – Looking Back
Smart Zone Lifestyle Competency

Old/Negative/Inappropriate Beliefs That Keep You Out of Your Smart Zone	Experiences/Contributing Factors
1.	1.
2.	2.
3.	3.
4.	4.
5.	5.

Identify Your Current Life Mode:
(The one you want to change/tells about the way you think)

Identify Your GPS Goals:
1.
2.
3.
4.
5.

Identify the Wisdom You Have Gained:

Fitness Management – Moving Forward
Smart Zone Lifestyle Competency

GPS Beliefs: Current/New Beliefs That Will Keep You in Your Smart Zone	Observations/Supporting Factors to Reinforce Beliefs
1.	1.
2.	2.
3.	3.
4.	4.
5.	5.

Build Your Smart Zone Life Mode:
(The one you want to have/your new way of thinking)

Identify Your Accountability Mechanisms:
1.
2.
3.
4.
5.

Identify Your Steps to Success:

Skill Management — Looking Back
Smart Zone Lifestyle Competency

Old/Negative/Inappropriate Beliefs That Keep You Out of Your Smart Zone	Experiences/Contributing Factors
1.	1.
2.	2.
3.	3.
4.	4.
5.	5.

Identify Your Current Life Mode:
(The one you want to change/tells about the way you think)

Identify Your GPS Goals:
1.
2.
3.
4.
5.

Identify the Wisdom You Have Gained:

Skill Management – Moving Forward
Smart Zone Lifestyle Competency

GPS Beliefs: Current/New Beliefs That Will Keep You in Your Smart Zone	Observations/Supporting Factors to Reinforce Beliefs
1.	1.
2.	2.
3.	3.
4.	4.
5.	5.

Build Your Smart Zone Life Mode:
(The one you want to have/your new way of thinking)

Identify Your Accountability Mechanisms:
1.
2.
3.
4.
5.

Identify Your Steps to Success:

Emotion Management – Looking Back
Smart Zone Lifestyle Competency

Old/Negative/Inappropriate Beliefs That Keep You Out of Your Smart Zone	Experiences/Contributing Factors
1.	1.
2.	2.
3.	3.
4.	4.
5.	5.

Identify Your Current Life Mode:
(The one you want to change/tells about the way you think)

Identify Your GPS Goals:
1.
2.
3.
4.
5.

Identify the Wisdom You Have Gained:

Emotion Management — Moving Forward
Smart Zone Lifestyle Competency

GPS Beliefs: Current/New Beliefs That Will Keep You in Your Smart Zone	Observations/Supporting Factors to Reinforce Beliefs
1.	1.
2.	2.
3.	3.
4.	4.
5.	5.

Build Your Smart Zone Life Mode:
(The one you want to have/your new way of thinking)

Identify Your Accountability Mechanisms:
1.
2.
3.
4.
5.

Identify Your Steps to Success:

Financial Management – Looking Back
Smart Zone Lifestyle Competency

Old/Negative/Inappropriate Beliefs That Keep You Out of Your Smart Zone	Experiences/Contributing Factors
1.	1.
2.	2.
3.	3.
4.	4.
5.	5.

Identify Your Current Life Mode:
(The one you want to change/tells about the way you think)

Identify Your GPS Goals:
1.
2.
3.
4.
5.

Identify the Wisdom You Have Gained:

✳

Financial Management — Moving Forward
Smart Zone Lifestyle Competency

GPS Beliefs: Current/New Beliefs That Will Keep You in Your Smart Zone	Observations/Supporting Factors to Reinforce Beliefs
1.	1.
2.	2.
3.	3.
4.	4.
5.	5.

Build Your Smart Zone Life Mode:
(The one you want to have/your new way of thinking)

Identify Your Accountability Mechanisms:
1.
2.
3.
4.
5.

Identify Your Steps to Success:

Daily Management – Looking Back
Smart Zone Lifestyle Competency

Old/Negative/Inappropriate Beliefs That Keep You Out of Your Smart Zone	Experiences/Contributing Factors
1.	1.
2.	2.
3.	3.
4.	4.
5.	5.

Identify Your Current Life Mode:
(The one you want to change/tells about the way you think)

Identify Your GPS Goals:
1.
2.
3.
4.
5.

Identify the Wisdom You Have Gained:

Daily Management – Moving Forward
Smart Zone Lifestyle Competency

GPS Beliefs: Current/New Beliefs That Will Keep You in Your Smart Zone	Observations/Supporting Factors to Reinforce Beliefs
1.	1.
2.	2.
3	3.
4.	4.
5.	5.

Build Your Smart Zone Life Mode:
(The one you want to have/your new way of thinking)

Identify Your Accountability Mechanisms:
1.
2.
3.
4.
5.

Identify Your Steps to Success:

Chapter 16

*6 Competencies for
a Business Person
in the Smart Zone*

To be a Business Person in the Smart Zone, there are 6 competencies that will get you there:

1. Business Management
2. Skill Management
3. Relationship Management
4. Knowledge Management
5. Mentor Management
6. Daily Management

Each of these competencies is essential to being in the Smart Zone. And you may have another competency you want to add that is essential to your own personal Smart Zone.

You will notice in the pages that follow that some of the competencies appear to overlap. As you begin to build your own Life Plan, ask yourself if the emphasis is on one competency more than the other. There really is no right answer.

These lists are not final. They are just a start and you may not agree with some of the points. Develop your own list to practice the competencies to keep you *Working in the Smart Zone.*

Each competency is explained on the following pages.

*

I. Business Management
This competency is related to the things you do to manage your business. You do not have to own your own business to manage your business.

For a *sales manager*, managing your business means:
- Keeping your content management system up to date
- Updating your business goals for this quarter
- Monitoring sales goal achievement

For a *midlevel manager*, managing your business means:
- Reading books about your field
- Knowing your "market" and your customer
- Studying your competitors

For a *service provider*, managing your business means:
- Studying the quarterly numbers
- Adjusting the next quarterly goals
- Remaining focused on customer satisfaction

To identify your own Business Management competencies ask yourself these five questions:
1. How do I measure my business success?
2. What actions do I need to take to manage my business well?
3. How will I know if I am managing my business better?
4. What resources do I need to help me manage my business better?
5. How can I improve my business management abilities?

2. Business Skill Management

This competency is related to the things you do to manage your specific skills as a business person.

For a *sales manager*, skill management means:

- Learning new negotiating techniques
- Improving your coaching skills
- Refining your presentation abilities

For a *midlevel manager*, skill management means:

- Attending a leadership seminar
- Role playing with a peer how to conduct a quarterly review with an employee
- Achieving required certifications within your field

For a *service provider*, skill management means:

- Managing your skills in customer service
- Improving your skills in conflict resolution
- Learning how to build a High Trust environment (Chapter 3: The Trust Factor)

To identify your own Business Skill Management competencies ask yourself these five questions:

1. How do I measure my business skills?
2. What actions do I need to take to manage my business skills well?
3. How will I know if I am managing my business skills better?
4. What resources do I need to help me manage my skills better?
5. How can I improve my business skills?

3. Business Relationship Management

This competency is related to the things you do to manage the relationships that are part of a successful business.

For a *sales manager*, relationship management means:
- Communicating frequently with other departments to maintain their support of sales
- Developing a system to keep your name in front of your product customers and to build relationships with your customers
- Creating an atmosphere of High Trust among sales staff to promote teamwork and focus on department sales goals

For a *midlevel manager*, relationship management means:
- Practicing the ability to maintain a level of satisfaction despite your differences with the staff you manage
- Creating ways your staff can build common ground

For a *service provider*, relationship management means:
- Managing your interpersonal skills with co-workers
- Learning to implement/build a High Trust environment (Chapter 3: The Trust Factor)

To identify your own Business Relationship Management competencies ask yourself these five questions:
1. How do I measure my business relationship success?
2. What actions do I need to take to manage my business relationships better?
3. How will I know if I am managing my business relationships well?
4. What resources do I need to help me manage my relationships better?
5. How can I improve my business relationships?

4. Business Knowledge Management

This competency is related to the things you do to manage your business knowledge.

For a *sales manager*, knowledge management means:

- Continually working to know your product fully
- Continually working to know your competitors' products to the full extent
- Working to know your industry trends
- Staying apprised of new codes, laws, and legislation related to your industry

For a *midlevel manager*, knowledge management means:

- Reading business books on leadership to help manage your staff
- Staying informed about the activities of your staff
- Working to know how your job function relates to customer and shareholder satisfaction.

For a *service provider*, knowledge management means:

- Taking courses to earn continuing education credits
- Reading journal articles in your field about upcoming technology

To identify your own Business Knowledge Management competencies ask yourself these five questions:

1. How do I measure my business knowledge success?
2. What actions do I need to take to manage my business knowledge better?
3. How will I know if I am managing my business knowledge well?
4. What resources do I need to help me manage my business knowledge better?
5. How can I improve my business knowledge?

5. Business Mentor Management

This competency is related to the business mentoring relationships you have.

For a *sales manager*, mentor management means:
- Identifying and building a mentor relationship with someone in your field
- Setting up a system of frequently working with your mentor

For a *midlevel manager*, mentor management means:
- Attending and participating in association meetings where you can meet and learn from people in your field with more experience
- Asking your immediate supervisor to mentor you in specific areas of your career

For a *service provider*, mentor management means:
- Meeting with others in your industry who are willing to be in a mentor relationship with you
- Identifying others in your field with more experience and studying their ideas and techniques

To identify your own Business Mentor Management competencies ask yourself these five questions:

1. How do I measure my business mentor success?
2. What actions do I need to take to manage my mentor relationships well?
3. How will I know if I am managing my business mentor relationship better?
4. What resources do I need to help me manage my mentor relationship better?
5. How can I improve my business mentor relationship?

6. Business Daily Management

This competency is related to your daily business management.

For a *sales manager*, daily management means:
- Preparing the night before for the next day's sales calls
- Being organized for your own productivity and to set an example for your sales staff
- Being responsible about using email so you are more efficient with your attention and energy

For a *midlevel manager*, daily management means:
- Setting aside 3 hours a week to work on the recruitment of additional staff rather than just waiting until someone resigns
- Holding staff meetings that are valuable by preparing an agenda emailing it to staff in advance

For a *service provider*, daily management means:
- Controlling daily stress that would interfere with customer interaction (Chapter 7: Managing Stress)
- Learning to have empathy for others in interactions (Chapter 12: Likeability)
- Utilizing a daily plan of goals to accomplish

To identify your own Business Daily Management competencies ask yourself these five questions:
1. How do I measure my daily management success?
2. What actions do I need to take to manage my daily business well?
3. How will I know if I am managing my daily business better?
4. What resources do I need to help me manage my daily business better?
5. How can I improve my daily management?

Chapter 17

*8 Competencies for
a Smart Zone Lifestyle*

To live a Smart Zone Lifestyle, there are 8 competencies that will get you there:

1. Self-Management
2. Health Management
3. Relationship Management
4. Fitness Management
5. Skill Management
6. Emotion Management
7. Financial Management
8. Daily Management

Each of these competencies is essential to living a Smart Zone Lifestyle. Again, you don't have to limit yourself to these eight. You may want to add another competency that is essential to your own personal Smart Zone. A Smart Zone Lifestyle will give you balance, improve your relationships, keep you productive, and lead to satisfaction in your life and in your work.

A Life Plan can be helpful for everyone, regardless of age, income, career, etc. The 8 Competencies for a Smart Zone Lifestyle will help you stay on target to live the way you intend. You will notice in the pages that follow that some of the competencies appear to overlap. As you begin to build your own Life Plan, ask yourself if the emphasis is on one competency more than the other. There really is no right answer as long as you include it under one competency.

This is not a final list. They are just a start and you may not agree with some of the points. Develop your own list to practice the competencies to keep you *Working in the Smart Zone.*

On the following pages each competency is explained.

I. Self-Management
This competency is related to the things you do daily to manage yourself, at work or at home.

To Live in the Smart Zone, Self-Management means:
- Managing your impulses so you don't overspend
- Setting up an organizational system so you can find your keys, your books, your BlackBerry, etc.
- Working to be on time for appointments
- Returning phone calls in a timely manner
- Limiting the amount of "junk" TV that you watch
- Making sure you keep your car maintained
- Preparing for events and appointments ahead of time
- Keeping one calendar of all your activities
- Managing your energy and attention to get things done so you are clearly focused (Chapter 1: The Smart Zone Model and How It Can Work for You)
- Keeping your home and work environments organized

To identify your own Self-Management competencies ask yourself these five questions:
1. How do I measure my self-management success?
2. What actions do I need to take to manage myself better?
3. How will I know if I am managing myself better?
4. What resources do I need to manage myself better?
5. How can I improve my self-management abilities?

2. Health Management

This competency is related to the things you do to manage your health. This is different from Fitness Management in that it relates to the quality of your health rather than your activities to get and remain fit.

To Live in the Smart Zone, Health Management means:
- Making and keeping appointments for yearly medical checkups
- Visiting the dentist regularly
- Eating healthy foods
- Wearing your safety belt in the car
- Wearing a helmet when you ride a bike
- Managing your stress level for health reasons (Chapter 7: Managing Stress)
- Getting an adequate amount of sleep regularly
- Learning your family history and your health risks
- Driving the speed limit and taking no unnecessary risks

To identify your own Health Management competencies ask yourself these five questions:
1. How do I measure my health management success?
2. What actions do I need to take to manage my health well?
3. How will I know if I am managing my health better?
4. What resources do I need to help me manage my health better?
5. How can I improve my health?

3. Relationship Management

This competency is related to the things you do to manage your relationships.

To Live in the Smart Zone, Relationship Management means:

- Putting notes in your calendar to contact people you care about (Chapter 28: Letter to Smart Zone Significants)
- Spending 10 minutes a day writing handwritten notes to people
- Having a get-together at your house so the people you know can get to know each other
- Spending time at a party getting to know people instead of spending the evening with just one person you see all the time
- Making a list of people's birthdays and surprising them on their birthdays
- Remembering important things about people you care about
- Going out with your spouse twice a month without your children
- Getting to know your children's friends

To identify your own Relationship Management competencies ask yourself these five questions:

1. How do I measure my relationship success?
2. What actions do I need to take to manage my relationships?
3. How will I know if I am managing my relationships better?
4. What resources do I need to help me manage my relationships better?
5. How can I improve my relationships?

4. Fitness Management

This competency is related to the things you do to get and stay fit. This is different from Health Management in that it relates to what you do to keep your body healthy.

To Live in the Smart Zone, Fitness Management means:

- Setting a plan to exercise aerobically at least 5 times a week for at least 30 minutes each time
- Lifting weights at least 3 times a week
- Developing accountability for exercise with a friend, trainer, or an exercise group (Chapter 19: Accountability Mechanisms)
- Subscribing to at least one magazine that will educate you in managing your fitness better
- Setting reasonable goals to build consistent fitness habits rather than looking for immediate results and doing too much too soon
- Varying your exercise routine so you don't get bored and so your body doesn't get used to just one thing
- Setting goals for fitness and tracking your progress
- Every day looking for 3 ways that you can increase your activity (e.g., take the stairs, park far away in a parking lot)

To identify your own Fitness Management competencies ask yourself these five questions:

1. How do I measure my fitness success?
2. What actions do I need to take to manage my fitness well?
3. How will I know if I am managing my fitness better?
4. What resources do I need to help me manage my fitness better?
5. How can I improve my fitness?

5. Skill Management

This competency is related to the things you do to improve your skills in your personal life.

To Live in the Smart Zone, Skill Management means:

- Learning how to use accounting software to manage your finances
- Learning how to install a faucet, change a light fixture, install a dimmer switch, repair a toilet
- Figuring out how to use an Excel spreadsheet to track home improvement projects
- Learning how to develop your own family website.
- Putting together a 1,000-piece puzzle
- Cooking a new recipe
- Learning how to repair a flat tire
- Planning a trip to a new destination
- Researching ways that you can save energy
- Figuring out how to use TiVo

To identify your own Skill Management competencies ask yourself these five questions:

1. How do I measure my skill success?
2. What actions do I need to take to manage my skills well?
3. How will I know if I am managing my skills better?
4. What resources do I need to help me manage my skills better?
5. How can I improve my skills?

6. Emotion Management
This competency is related to the things you do to manage your emotions.

To Live in the Smart Zone, Emotion Management means:
- Working to improve your ability to perceive the emotions of others (Chapter 2: Emotional Intelligence)
- Managing your own emotions (Chapter 2: Emotional Intelligence)
- Learning to be Snow White (Chapter 5: Communication)
- Learning to express yourself effectively through your words rather than through your behavior
- Learning to manage stress and anger (Chapter 7: Managing Stress)
- Being able to discuss high-conflict subjects
- Being able to turn "unknowns" into "knowns" by using the "What I Know For Sure" exercise (Chapter 27: What I Know For Sure)
- Working to increase your own Emotional Intelligence (Chapter 2: Emotional Intelligence)
- Increasing optimism and happiness in your environment (Chapter 10: Managing Mood)
- Increasing self-awareness and improving interpersonally (Chapter 2: Emotional Intelligence)

To identify your own Emotion Management competencies ask yourself these five questions:
1. How do I measure my emotional success?
2. What actions do I need to take to manage my emotions well?
3. How will I know if I am managing my emotions better?
4. What resources do I need to help me manage my emotions better?
5. How can I improve my emotional abilities?

7. Financial Management

This competency is related to the things you do to manage your finances.

To Live in the Smart Zone, Financial Management means:

- Having a system to know the status of your finances at all times
- Maximizing your 401(k)
- Planning for retirement
- Minimizing the use of credit cards
- Knowing your credit score and checking it twice a year
- Researching ways to manage your finances
- Attending seminars about financial management
- Joining an investment group
- Checking your credit card statements and making sure all charges are yours
- Paying in cash whenever possible

To identify your own Financial Management competencies ask yourself these five questions:

1. How do I measure my financial success?
2. What actions do I need to take to manage my finances well?
3. How will I know if I am managing my finances better?
4. What resources do I need to help me manage my finances better?
5. How can I improve my finances?

8. Daily Management

This competency is related to the things you do to manage yourself daily.

To Live in the Smart Zone, Daily Management means:

- Planning ahead
- Being solution oriented (Chapter 6: Solution Oriented)
- Learning to manage stress to minimize exaggerated responses (Chapter 7: Managing Stress)
- Being willing to manage perceptions and being open to the influence of others (Chapter 4: Managing Perception)
- Building a High Trust environment with those you interact with daily (Chapter 3: The Trust Factor)
- Living a life of integrity, responsibility, and managing energy and attention (Chapter 11: Sanity Sustained)
- Choosing one of the 15 EQ factors each week and working to build your EQ skills (Chapter 2: Emotional Intelligence)
- Doing things that contribute a sense of optimism and happiness to your environment (Chapter 10: Managing Mood)
- Improving your ability to communicate with other people using the Smart Sandwich Model (Chapter 5: Communication)

To identify your own Daily Management competencies ask yourself these five questions:

1. How do I measure my daily success?
2. What actions do I need to take to manage myself well?
3. How will I know if I am managing myself better?
4. What resources do I need to help me manage myself better?
5. How can I improve myself?

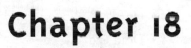

Chapter 18

Smart Zone Thinking

In the Smart Zone Life Plan, there is an opportunity to identify your faulty thinking and to identify your new way of thinking; the one you want to have. The new way of thinking is your Smart Zone Life Mode.

As you develop your Life Plan, work to develop your own Smart Zone thinking by using the following guide:

Looking Back: Faulty Thinking

Looking Back involves the type of thinking that may be your current life mode. This type of thinking is the type you want to change. Your current life mode tells about the way you think. It is important to be aware of your faulty thinking.

The type of thinking that is faulty has the following characteristics:

- Problem focused
- Negative
- Self-defeating
- Hopeless
- Dead-end

Moving Forward: Smart Zone Thinking

Moving Forward involves the type of thinking that is Smart Zone thinking, which is what you want as your current life mode. Moving Forward thinking allows you to be *Working in Your Smart Zone.*

Smart Zone thinking has the following characteristics:

- Solution focused
- Positive
- Builds on your strengths
- Hopeful
- Open-ended, considering many possibilities

When you are developing your Life Plan, it is important to recognize that Smart Zone thinking also includes one of the most important characteristics of Emotional Intelligence: Empathy.

※

How to Think with Empathy—Not Wimpathy

Empathy is the awareness of the feelings, needs and concerns of others. Research in the 1970s and 1980s suggested that there was a negative correlation between positions of authority and empathetic abilities. But this attitude is no longer effective for organizations. We work in a team-oriented business culture requiring group cooperation.

Thinking with empathy enables us to strengthen relationships, pick up early warning signs and recognize opportunities to influence others.

Many may feel that showing empathy weakens your authority. In some cases this is true. A lawyer showing empathy for opposing council will not strengthen his case. At times it is necessary to talk straight and hold someone accountable rather than empathize.

Sympathy can be mistaken for *empathy*. Sympathy is when you feel compassion for someone, but this is your feeling only and does not focus on what others are feeling. Keep this in mind. People in the Smart Zone think with empathy.

Here are five Smart Ideas for how to have empathetic thinking:

- **Think before acting and listen well.** Listening is an art, but it also has a financial impact. Studies show that physicians who listen to their patients for at least 3 minutes have significantly fewer malpractice lawsuits against them. When we are too eager to make a sale or get our point across we are less likely to listen well. The next time someone objects to what you think, resist the urge to defend your point and try responding with these words, "You're absolutely right, I should consider that."

- **Don't be fake.** Have integrity. Empathizing with understanding someone's point of view doesn't mean you have to agree with it. In business negotiations when we understand how the other party feels it doesn't mean we give in. It simply means we can be more skillful in our negotiation and minimize resentment and ill will.

- **No "one-upping."** Try not to always project your thoughts onto others. It is human nature to respond to someone else's problem with an experience we have had. To lead with empathy hear out what others are saying without sharing a personal story to "one-up" theirs. Don't go on and on about your situation. Make the other person important.

- **You don't have to solve it.** Just acknowledging someone's problem or point of view is sometimes all that is needed. Whether or not you solve the problem, just showing concern and making a goodwill effort to make things better does some good for the other person emotionally. People need to know that you feel their pain.

- **Watch out for empathy distress.** Sometimes called "compassion fatigue," empathy distress is when people suffer from someone else's pain and suffering. Medical and social services workers are especially prone to this, as are customer service representatives who deal with unhappy customers all day. Even in an office environment when a co-worker is faced with being laid off we may begin to feel the anxiety and stress for them. To combat empathy distress, stay open to your feelings and don't blame yourself for negative outcomes of others. Know the boundary.

The Empathy Quiz

Take this quick empathy quiz. Draw the letter "E" on your forehead. Based on a study by Adam Galinsky, PhD, a social psychologist at Northwestern University, if you drew the "E" so that it would appear backwards to others, you are less likely to consider the viewpoints of others. But if you drew the "E" backward so that it would appear legible to others, you are more likely to consider others' viewpoints.

My First Day Working for Dr. Phil

My first day working for Phillip C. McGraw, Ph.D., also known as Dr. Phil, shows the power of thinking in the Smart Zone.

As the story goes, I first met Phil in 1997. At the time, he was working on the Oprah trial but in our meeting he didn't give me many details. All I knew was that he had formed a company, Courtroom Sciences, Inc. and he had a professional staff assisting attorneys with litigation. In 1997, I was building my clinical and consulting practice and wasn't looking for another career. I was interested in talking with him about some contract work. He was interested in me for a full-time position.

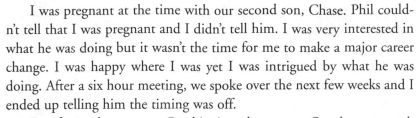

I was pregnant at the time with our second son, Chase. Phil couldn't tell that I was pregnant and I didn't tell him. I was very interested in what he was doing but it wasn't the time for me to make a major career change. I was happy where I was yet I was intrigued by what he was doing. After a six hour meeting, we spoke over the next few weeks and I ended up telling him the timing was off.

Fast forward two years. By this time, he was on Oprah every week and there was a story in the *Dallas Morning News* about his success. He had written his first book and it was clear that the Oprah trial was the litigation he had been involved in when I'd met him two years earlier. While I was impressed that he was now "Dr. Phil," I was even more impressed with how he had grown Courtroom Sciences.

I wrote him a quick note that said:

> *"Congratulations on your success. If you ever need a good shrink, give me a call."*
>
> —*Susan Fletcher, Ph.D.*

He responded.

Two days later he called me himself, and at first I thought my office manager was joking with me. I expected my husband's voice when I picked up the line on hold. No mistake. It was Phil's voice and not my husband's attempt at an impersonation.

When I wrote the note, I didn't expect a response. After all, he was famous, busy, and probably had written me off a long time ago as someone who couldn't make up her mind—someone who didn't know what she wanted to be when she grew up. I was caught off guard as we talked about why he called.

We talked for a few minutes and at first I was casual. He told me he had gotten my note and he wanted to follow up. I teased him that I thought he could use some appointments for therapy and I could try and fit him in next week. Luckily he laughed. Then he told me he was calling because he was interested in talking to me about whether my timing was better now. He wanted to know if I was interested in talking again about working at Courtroom Sciences.

I had always wondered what it would be like to work there. I felt like I'd missed a chance to be a part of something big that made a difference in people's lives. It was also attractive to think about working as part of his team. The people on his staff were what others call "wicked smart" and the professionalism was attractive to me.

We met two weeks later, this time for most of the day, and he showed me around his office. Many of the associates were traveling working on trials all across the country. Phil introduced me to his business partner, Gary Dobbs, and he talked about his vision for the company. I liked that he had carved out a place for my expertise. He liked that I was a strong woman with the ability to speak in front of people and be quick on my feet. At the end of that day, my husband and I talked seriously about what would be involved if I took the offer.

My husband, an engineer, built a spreadsheet with all of the costs that needed to be considered. I would have to close my practice allowing time for the other therapists to find another place to be. I had a lease on office space I would need to renegotiate, and I would have a longer commute from Plano to Las Colinas. We considered all the costs as we got it down on paper.

I did a lot of preparation to get ready to talk about the possibility of working for Phil. I did a lot of thinking—Moving Forward thinking— as I carefully considered the opportunity.

Phil and I came to an agreement and he designated my first day as two weeks later. He told me he was eager to get me started because there were some big cases in progress that he wanted me to get involved in as quickly as possible.

On my first day, I arrived early and Phil met me in the lobby. I was nervous but also excited about the opportunity. It felt like a good fit and I was glad I had done all the necessary Smart Zone thinking to be ready to begin.

Phil showed me to my office. The name plate, business cards, files, and a Visa card all bore my name. It was if they had been waiting a long time for me to arrive. They seemed so prepared and I remember telling myself, "I made the right decision." Phil left me alone to review some papers and I got cozy in my new big chair. It was only a few minutes later that I realized one piece of preparation had been overlooked.

A woman named Beth walked by the office door and almost without looking said, "Good morning." "Good morning," I responded automatically. That obviously threw her off, because she stepped back to the open door of my office. She asked me where Meredith was and I told her I wasn't sure. I abruptly introduced myself and told her that this was my first day and I hadn't met everyone yet. I could tell from Beth's facial expression that something was not adding up. I needed to make sure I kept moving in the direction of Smart Zone thinking.

Beth explained that I was in Meredith's office and that she hadn't heard that Phil was hiring more staff. My arrival had been unexpected and she was just concerned about where Meredith had been moved.

I eventually found out that Meredith's last day had been the Friday before. Unfortunately, though, the staff hadn't been told.

To their credit, the administrative staff at Courtroom Sciences was very prepared for my arrival—they had ordered business cards in advance, had prepared the office for my arrival, and had even ordered me my own Visa card. The staff, however, had not been prepared for my arrival. It was clear to me that Meredith was well liked by the staff. Their thinking was, "Susan has taken Meredith's job."

Although I never understood what really happened or the reasons Meredith was no longer working there, the bottom line was that Meredith was no longer on staff, and even though I'd never even met her I seemed to get the blame for her sudden departure.

This was one of the hardest times that I've ever had keeping myself thinking in the Smart Zone. After all, I had been thinking about this job for two years and my husband and I had weighed all the angles to make sure this was the kind of move I wanted to make. Phil had been so deliberate about recruiting me a second time, especially since I had turned him down once. I got the feeling that very few people turned Phil down.

It took about three months for me to overcome the Meredith situation, and I only got through it by using Smart Zone thinking—I showed empathy for Meredith without engaging in too much conversation about her departure. I worked to remain hopeful and solution oriented in the way I got to know people and worked with the staff. I worked hard to remain positive and open-ended in the way I approached my growth in the company. I tried to build on my strengths and recognized that they had to decide to accept me. I worked to build trust and used my skills of Emotional Intelligence.

I worked at Courtroom Sciences for almost a year. Ironically I left my position because I became pregnant with my third child, Sam. The pace of the position was too much for a woman who was pregnant, and I enjoyed a boring but peaceful bed rest for almost four months. As I re-evaluated my desire to go back into my clinical practice and build my consulting and speaking business, I appreciated what I had learned about myself and how I had used Smart Zone thinking to *Work in my Smart Zone.*

Chapter 19

Accountability
Mechanisms

Accountability Partners are those people or systems you have put in place to catch you when you deviate from your Smart Zone Life Plan. In the Moving Forward section of the Smart Zone Life Plan, there is a place to identify your Accountability Mechanisms. By developing Accountability Mechanisms with a partner you are developing a way to build self-trust and to use the trust you have in others to hold you to the goal.

> *"Don't make friends who are comfortable to be with.*
> *Make friends who will force you to lever yourself up."*
> – Thomas Watson, founder of IBM

What to Consider When it Comes to Accountability

To follow your GPS Beliefs and be successful, it is important to have Accountability Partners. The Accountability Mechanisms that you identify are designed to ensure that you maintain your new Life Path and achieve success. Here are some Smart Ideas you can use to develop your Accountability System as part of a Smart Zone Life Plan:

- Establish a partner to check in with regularly about your progress and direction on your life plan. This person could be a colleague you trust with the information in your Life Plan.

- Develop a standard set of questions with your Accountability Partner that you will answer honestly that will reveal your true direction and success in making the change.

- Speak with your Accountability Partner monthly.

- Write down what you are being held accountable for and keep it where you can see it.

- Remember: an Accountability Partner is only as effective as you make him or her.

- Hold yourself accountable as much as possible and report regularly to your partner.

Ways to Build Accountability in the Workplace

Holding people accountable is one way to build trust in a work environment. Expectations need to be clarified and accountability needs to be present. Without accountability, it is possible for people to "quit and stay." When people quit and stay they tend to give up at work and do the minimum tasks to stay productive. Here are some Smart Ideas for practicing workplace accountability:

- Hold regular staff meetings
- Nip bad behavior, negativity and blame in the bud
- Reward good behavior
- Live by example
- Don't over promise
- Be realistic about your abilities
- Be willing to ask for help

How to Know When You are Not Getting the Value

You must be willing to be honest with your Accountability Partner. Here are some ways that you know that you are not getting the value with your accountability mechanism:

- You miss scheduled meetings with your accountability partner
- Your partner doesn't hold you accountable (find another partner—and quickly!)
- You are not progressing in your Life Plan
- You can't think of anything to talk about
- You have trouble talking about the bad stuff and only report the good stuff
- You find yourself dreading the upcoming conversations

Chapter 20

Intentional Success

Someone once asked: "Are successful people smart or just lucky?" I know the answer. Successful people are smart enough to know when they are lucky. I believe they have Intentional Success.

What is Intentional Success?

Intentional Success is planned success—the kind you write about in your Smart Zone Life Plan. It is the kind of success that is deliberate and well thought out. A Life Plan is like a business plan. You look at it as a means to an end. You have to know where you are going to get you there. It is not likely to happen with just luck.

In this chapter, you will learn a few ways to help you continue on a path of Intentional Success. You will learn about eliminating toxic influences, getting in the flow, using the Smart Sandwich Model to communicate and getting engaged. All of these are ways to keep you *Working in the Smart Zone.*

Eliminating Toxic Influences

One of the important components to Intentional Success is to eliminate toxic influences. In our clinical practice, we use this terminology all the time. When I use it in a corporate environment, the first response I hear is that it is impossible to eliminate toxic influences because you can't pick your boss and you can't always pick the people you work with. Well, think about it again. You can't always walk away from other toxic influences, either—your parents, your spouse, or your customers—and you are in trouble if you think you can eliminate your business partner. Instead of eliminating a toxic person, you have to be able to eliminate the toxicity of their influence.

It is a constant struggle, I admit, for me as well. In a workplace, it means you may be dealing with the following scenarios:

> Kathi likes being a graphic designer but she gets easily frustrated by customers expecting that changes should take her only a minute. They get surprised when they see the bill for the time it took her to do her work. She finds herself getting frustrated all the time with what on the surface might be ignorance on the part of the cus-

tomer. She finds herself influenced by the toxicity of the relationship.

Taylor is a practicing physician who enjoys her job. The part she doesn't like is the billing and preapproval with managed care. Early in her career, it was a lot easier to treat patients the way they needed to be treated. She finds herself influenced by the toxicity of the system.

William is pleased with his promotion to managing the southern region for his company. He was ready for a change and he welcomed the additional responsibility. After three weeks in the new position, he traveled six times to different parts of his territory. He finds himself influenced by the toxicity of the responsibilities.

Paul has been in sales for his whole career. Every time he changes companies, it is like a promotion. He enjoys the challenge and the newness of the position. The only problem he continually faces is that each company has its own system for reporting and managing contacts. His colleagues are not open to his suggestions for change to bring their technology into this century. He finds himself influenced by the toxicity of the backwards nature of his new company.

Gordon has always liked his boss. He has felt he has been fair to him in the past and always set him up to be successful. Now Gordon's boss is going through a divorce and he seems to have become disengaged at work. This leaves Gordon hanging because he no longer has an accurate pipeline to know what is going on in the company or where he stands in relation to his peers. He finds himself influenced by the toxicity of his deteriorating relationship with his boss.

Kathi, Taylor, William, Paul, and Gordon are all affected by the influence of what is going on around them. It is difficult for each to see their way out of the toxicity without something outside of them changing. People in the Smart Zone understand that it is not a waiting game for something to change. It is through Intentional Success and working on your GPS beliefs that you have the opportunity to evoke change and eliminate the toxicity. Even with the presence of toxicity, one of the ways you can achieve intentional success is to get in the flow.

Getting in the Flow

Do you know anyone who makes a difficult task look easy? Like my husband, for example, who can simply take something apart when it stops working, fiddle with all the wires and things and get it to start working again just like new. It may be because he is in "flow." Flow actually affects our brain activity. When we are in flow, we can be engaged in an exceptionally demanding task and yet our brain is operating with a minimal expenditure of energy that is more efficient and precise.

When you are following the flow you will feel passionate about the task at hand. Have you ever been late getting home for dinner because you were shooting hoops and lost track of time? Or wondered where the day went after shopping with a friend? If so, you were in flow.

In a recent issue of *Fast Company* magazine the CEO of grocery chain Whole Foods Markets, John Mackey, announced that he will now reduce his salary to $1. He went on to say that he is financially secure and no longer wants to work for money, "but simply for the joy of the work itself..." (*Fast Company*, February, 2007) That is flow! People in the Smart Zone can have this type of focus and enjoyment at work, even if they are depending on the paycheck to pay their bills. It is a step towards developing Intentional Success. Here's how:

- **Use Your Intuition.** Part of following the flow is developing your intuition. Intuition is that sixth sense that enables us to size up a situation correctly without the conscious use of reasoning. It's when you have a "hunch" and want to hire someone after you've spoken to them for only 10 minutes. Or when you think, "I really don't think we should buy from this vendor." Listening to your gut feelings will put you in the flow faster.

- **Be Present.** Being present begins with self-awareness. People that are self-aware are also aware of others. Have you ever happened upon a co-worker sitting at her desk all clenched up with a scowl on her face over a project deadline? Relax and be sympathetic to your co-worker's anxiety by saying, "What's going on? Is something wrong?" Be sympathetic and ask some detailed questions about the task, make a small joke and maybe suggest a creative idea. But don't gripe! Be sensitive about how you would feel in the same situation.

- **Devote Your Energy to the Task at Hand.** Make a point of focusing on one thing at a time. Multitasking moves us out of the flow. Don't have an important conversation with a co-worker while making copies at the copy machine. Put away your BlackBerry while working on a task. Immerse yourself in whatever you are doing.

- **When Flow Slows.** When our job lacks flow we get bored. Ever answer phone calls from headhunters even though you don't want a new job? When your flow slows it's time to refine your skills. Create your own challenges at work that go beyond your job requirements. Can you finish that report faster? Can you call on five instead of four customers a day? Can you save an extra few dollars from some of your suppliers? Now create your own personal best and try to beat it!

- **Don't be a Flow Buster!** The "it's my way or the highway" attitude moves everyone in the organization out of the flow. I once consulted with a Fortune 30 company whose Vice President would solicit his managers' input and then blast them in front of the group if he didn't like their ideas. Respect the fact that everyone approaches a task differently and that the successful outcome is where the focus must be. In a recent article in *Entrepreneur* magazine Trudy Bourgeois, author of *The Hybrid Leader*, was quoted as saying that one trait that younger workers look for in leaders is respect for their individuality. Sometimes it takes only one bad experience to quash one's inner voice of intuition and make it harder to move back into the flow.

The Smart Sandwich Way to Communicate

When I consult with key leaders I find they often want to discuss how to communicate effectively with their supervisees, co-workers and higher ups. They want to be intentional about how they communicate instead of leaving effective communication up to chance. I quickly realized that one strategy we use in our clinical practice would be beneficial in a corporate environment. Communicating is communicating, no matter what the subject. We covered the Smart Sandwich way to communicate in *Parenting in the Smart Zone* and now we are pleased to help you have intentional success in the workplace using the same technique—with a twist: a structure for communication that brings Intentional Success, called the Smart Sandwich Model of communication.

SMART Sandwich

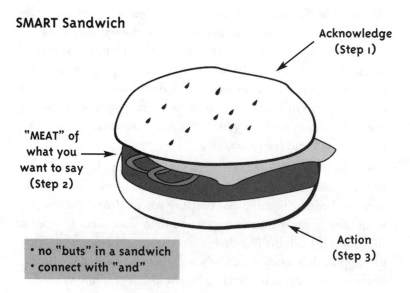

The Smart Sandwich Model has three steps that can be used to communication intentionally:

Step One: Communicate some acknowledgement

People tend to repeat themselves when they don't feel that they have been heard. Again, people tend to repeat themselves when they don't feel that they have been heard. If you acknowledge or validate the expected response first, it will go a long way in helping with conflict, especially in a work environment focusing on productive communication.

Step Two: Communicate the most important information in 15 seconds

By identifying the meat of what you want to say, you pinpoint really quickly what needs to be communicated. By using the Smart Sandwich model you can effectively communicate without a lot of fluff that takes so long that the message is lost. Being able to communicate, whether it is with preferences or feelings, contributes to a well-developed emotional intelligence.

Step Three: Create the opportunity to manage conflict

This is the action part of the model. As most adults can attest, conflict is difficult to manage in any relationship, especially a working relationship, if an action step is not involved. However, an action step is what most people tend to leave out, creating an environment where the communication becomes circular and redundant. It is difficult to accomplish much of anything if the suggestion of action is not made.

Here is an example of how the Smart Sandwich Model can apply in the workplace between a manager and a supervisee:

> *Manager: Wayne, you were late on this deadline and we really needed your ideas from yesterday's meeting today.*
>
> *Wayne: I know you expected it would have been completed by now.* (Step One)
>
> *I worked on it most of last night and this morning and I'm having difficulty getting the ideas for the proposal on paper.* (Step Two)
>
> *I talked to Jack before lunch and that will help me produce what you needed. Would it be possible for me to send you what I have right now and*

then you and I could talk about it for a few minutes? I want to make sure that it hits the mark and I am willing to work on it as long as it takes to get it done correctly. Next time at the end of a meeting it would be helpful for us to have a flipchart and write down some ideas so we can review them before the meeting ends. I want to make sure I always am able to complete the work in a timely manner. (Step Three)

The expectation would be that the focus would be on the action rather than the "meat."

Without using the Smart Sandwich Model, another type of interaction could go like this:

Boss: Catherine: I'm really frustrated that you continue to miss your sales targets. You are doing a good job but you aren't meeting your goals.

Using the Smart Sandwich Model, the communication can be much more effective, like this:

Boss: Catherine: I know you have only been with us six months and you are improving your sales every month. I can see that you are putting forth a lot of effort. (Step One)

You are still not meeting the projected number of sales and I am concerned that you are not building enough contacts to be able to generate the number of sales expected. (Step Two)

What are some things you can do in the next 30 days to generate more sales? I would also like you to come up with a plan of other ways to generate more sales so the numbers next month improve. (Step Three)

When you communicate using the Smart Sandwich Model, eliminate the word "but" and instead use the word "and." The word "but" negates everything you said right before that. It also tends to encourage defensiveness that might make it hard for someone to hear the meat of what you want to say and the action plan. Both "and" and "but" are connectors. This technique is also very useful with other types of communication, even when you're communicating with your spouse and children. It will give you Intentional Success to communicate in the Smart Zone.

What it Really Means to Get Engaged

When considering Intentional Success, it is important to understand the concept of engagement. Engaged employees have passion for their work and their organization. Companies with engaged employees are up to 38% more productive. Therefore, employees are the greatest source of productivity improvement in your organization.

An engaged employee can have an enormous impact on an organization. Are you an engaged employee? Do you think the people in your organization are giving it their all? Do you think employees in your company feel appreciated and look forward to coming to work each day? If you answered "No" to any of these questions then your company could be missing out. Companies with engaged employees have 40% more profitability, 50% lower turnover, 56% more loyal customers, and are 38% more likely to have above-average productivity.

According to The Center for Creative Leadership, "Among the factors that lead to 'engagement' are supervisors who show they care by praising and encouraging both growth and at-work friendship."

Organizations in the Smart Zone have engaged employees and leaders. Here are some Smart Ideas to help you and your organization become more engaged, leading to a greater chance for Intentional Success:

- **Be a "can do" person.** Instead of focusing on what you cannot do, focus on what you *can* do. Be action oriented. Many times people don't take action because they believe they aren't worth much. Our beliefs affect the way we feel, which affects the way we think, which affects the way we act (Chapter 7: Managing Stress). So the next time a co-worker asks you to help organize a customer appreciation day, instead of saying, "No, I *can't* do that," say, "***What I can do is*** coordinate the customer invitations."

- **Get to know people.** Learn what excites your employees, co-workers and customers. What are their goals? What stresses them out? How do they define success? I don't suggest prying too deeply into a personal conversation. Just show an appropriate and genuine interest in your colleagues and their well-being.

- **Use meaningful rewards and recognition.** An employee appreciation golf outing on a Saturday might not feel rewarding to a single parent who has young children. Also, recognize the efforts and accomplishments of those working on long-term projects to give them a boost towards achieving their goal.

- **Say "goodbye" to blame.** The process of figuring out who to blame is a time waster. Mistakes should be accepted and encouraged. Mistakes show that action was being sought. We can't all hit the bulls-eye every time. When things go wrong, ask "what" and "how" questions like, "What can we do in the future?" or "How can we change what has occurred?"

By getting in the mindset of Intentional Success, you are well on your way to *Working in the Smart Zone.*

Chapter 21

*My Day/Week in
the Smart Zone*

To keep yourself in the Smart Zone, build your decisions around how you want to spend your day. Each week should contribute to the goal of staying in the Smart Zone. Work your way to being more productive and satisfied every day. First outline your activities for each morning, afternoon, and evening. Then for each day fill in which of your *6 Competencies for a Business Person* in the Smart Zone and your *8 Competencies of a Smart Zone Lifestyle* are included (see figure next page).

What follows on the next few pages is a sample Day/Week in the Smart Zone profile for a sales manager. Also in this chapter is a sample profile that you can use to build your own Day/Week in the Smart Zone worksheet. If you would like additional Day/Week in the Smart Zone worksheets, email your request to us at Susan@SmartZoneExpert.com. Put in the subject line: "Day/Week in the Smart Zone Profile Worksheet" and we'll be happy to send you the Word templates.

	Lifestyle Competency	Business Competency
Business Management (BM)		X
Relationship Management (RM)	X	X
Knowledge Management (KM)		X
Mentor Management (MM)		X
Self-Management (SfM)	X	
Health Management (HM)	X	
Fitness Management (FtM)	X	
Skill Management (SkM)	X	X
Emotion Management (EM)	X	
Financial Management (FnM)	X	
Daily Management (DM)	X	X

Sample Profile: Sales Manager

Day	Morning	Afternoon
Sunday	Church, Breakfast with the family	Family activity (lake, movie, game), Work out, chores around the house
Monday	Work out; Kids to school; Prospect; Sales Calls; Sales Team Management	Meetings; Reach out to Mentors & Accountability Partners
Tuesday	Work out; Take the kids to school; Staff meeting	Read & Research; Marketing; Sales Team Management
Wednesday	Work out; Take the kids to school; Prospect; Sales Calls	Product Development; Marketing; Business Lunch with Mentor; Sales Team Management
Thursday	Work out; Sales Calls Manage Finances; Sales Team Management	Product Development; Read knowledge-based materials
Friday	Work out; Take the kids to school; Account Management	Account Management; Customer Lunch; Late afternoon to myself
Saturday	Work out; Sports activities and chores	Sports activities and chores

Evening	Competency
Get ready for the week ahead	FtM–Life DM–Life/Bus SfM–Life RM–Life/Bus
Home with family	FtM–Life DM–Life/Bus MM–Bus
Coach Soccer Practice	FtM–Life DM–Life/Bus SkM–Life/Bus BM–Bus
Business Dinner with Wife Included	FtM–Life DM–Life/Bus MM–Bus RM–Life/Bus
Home with family	FtM–Life DM–Life/Bus FnM–Life KM–Bus
Do some activity with the family	FtM–Life DM–Life/Bus HM–Life RM–Life/Bus EM–Life
Out with friends or other couples	FtM–Life DM–Life/Bus RM–Life/Bus EM–Life

Day/Week in the Smart Zone

Day	Morning	Afternoon
Sunday		
Monday		
Tuesday		
Wednesday		
Thursday		
Friday		
Saturday		

Evening	Competency

Chapter 22

Generation Smart Zone

Do you find it a challenge to work with people of different ages within your organization? The ways different generations react to authority and work/life rules can cause conflict. As a Mother's Day gift my husband recently took me to see The Police in concert in Dallas. At the concert I noticed people of all ages. Isn't it amazing how some music crosses the lines between generations? Even if you aren't Sting, this type of broad generational appeal is critical to maximize the success and productivity of your organization.

Most companies in America are facing the issue of managing generational differences. Which generation are you?

Table of Generational Differences	
Traditionalists **Birth Years 1925 to 1945**	Known as the "Silent Generation," traditionalists have a "We will prevail" attitude and are characterized by loyalty, duty and conformity. Some may see them as rigid and dictatorial.
Baby Boomers **Birth Years 1946 to 1960**	This generation has been called the "Me Generation" and enjoys being involved, valued and needed. Boomers are optimistic and strive to find fulfillment at work. They are willing to work all hours, often taking it to the workaholic level. I know a lot of people like this-how about you?
Generation X (this is me! I barely made it) **Birth Years 1961 to 1980**	Famous for being latchkey kids, I call this the "What about me?" generation. Gen X'ers are characterized as independent and resourceful, and value a network of close, reliable friends. Some may view them as impatient and willing to throw out tried-and-true strategies.
Generation Y/ Millennials **Birth Years 1981 to Present**	This techno-savvy generation has never known life without computers and grew up in an atmosphere of diversity and collaboration. They expect to have input in all decisions affecting their work, and accept working with people of many cultures, races and lifestyles. Some may see them as self-absorbed and spoiled. Parents today need to work to keep their kids grounded.

People in the Smart Zone can work effectively with all generations-no matter what. Smart Zone strategies teach us how to use our own emotional skills to interact with others in a productive manner.

Here are some Smart Ideas for dealing with different generations in your organization:

How to work with a Traditionalist (ages 60 to 80). Even if you are the boss, the traditionalist may speak to you in a parental tone. Traditionalists are nearing the end of their careers. Show respect for their experience and incorporate their advice. Say things like, "Your experience is respected," and "It is valuable to hear what has worked in the past."

How to work with a Baby Boomer (ages 45 to 60). Boomers value the title, office and influence they have. They will be motivated by how worthy a special task makes them feel—especially if it benefits society at large. To motivate a baby boomer use phrases like, "You are valuable," "Your opinion is worth a lot," and "Your contribution is unique and important to our success."

How to work with a Gen X'er (ages 25 to 45). Know that Gen X'ers are less likely to sacrifice personal time for the good of the company. Gen X'ers value the personal growth that they will experience from their job and work assignments. They are looking for ways to make themselves more valuable and marketable. Stay in the Smart Zone by approaching them with comments like, "Let's explore some options outside of the box," and "Your technical expertise is a big asset." They feel rewarded when they are given the opportunity to learn a new skill.

How to work with a Millennial/Gen Y'er (ages 18 to 25). Accustomed to being multi-taskers and being quickly accessible through email and/or a cell phone, the Millennials will be equally as busy outside of work. They are motivated by knowing their input and opinion matters—and expect to be involved in decisions. The "it's my way or the highway" approach will shut them down. Stay in the Smart Zone by using statements like, "You will be collaborating with other bright, creative people," and "You have really rescued this situation with your commitment."

For all generations, focus on:
• fairness

• growth

• opportunity

These three ingredients are NOT generationally specific, according to a recent article in *Fast Company*. Every person wants to be treated fairly, to feel that they are continuing to learn and grow, and to have a sense of purpose in life. By following these tips you can continue *Working in the Smart Zone*.

Chapter 23

*A Crisis is a Terrible
Thing to Waste*

"Only those who fail greatly can ever achieve greatly."
– President John F. Kennedy

Life is What Happens When You Plan for Something Else

A few months ago I spent some time in a "crisis mode." Our busy work schedule was changed midstream when a deadline was moved up, a client had a crisis with a key leader's resignation, my son came down with the flu and my father had a major complication during heart bypass surgery in Florida. We triaged my responsibilities and I took an emergency trip to Florida to be with my family. Thankfully I could be with them while my dad began his recovery, and he is now doing well.

We all have times when we shift into crisis mode. It happens when your car won't start and you're late to an important meeting. A tough deadline at work gets pushed up. Your company is about to lose a huge customer. An employee you're depending on quits. An OSHA inspector shows up unannounced. By staying in the Smart Zone you can get through a crisis mode and come out better for it.

During a crisis our brain falls back on simple, sometimes primitive, responses and puts aside complex thought. All focus is on the urgent present crisis. We were all horrified when a Minnesota bridge collapsed, claiming many lives and injuring many people. This crisis brought to light that there are more than 70,000 bridges in the U.S. rated "structurally deficient" and prompted an immediate assessment of Minnesota's emergency response system. In addition it spurred a long-overdue mandate for inspections of bridges all over the country. As a result, it is very possible that safety standards for our roads and bridges will improve, benefiting all of us. Once a crisis is over, our problem solving can turn a crisis into improved standards, improved conditions, improved safety, and one of the best opportunities for improvement.

Here are Smart Ideas for using crisis mode to your advantage:

- **Make a wrong right.** When a mistake is made, admit it instead of covering it up. Trust is built when you are honest and accept responsibility to make it right. Blaming others, not responding, and refusing to take responsibility create a lack of trust and discredit you. Everyone makes mistakes. It is how you respond when a mistake is made that makes the difference.

- **Don't kill the guy who does your oil change.** Have you ever seen someone throwing a fit at the car repair shop because their oil change wasn't done in one hour? I call this an exaggerated response. Our body doesn't know the difference between work stress, home stress and personal stress. When we have too much stress our stress hormones kick in, causing a small hassle to suddenly be overwhelming. Learn to recognize when your stress level is getting high and discipline yourself to eliminate it. You could exercise, go shopping, get more sleep, read a book, surf the internet, call a co-worker or friend, or leave the office for lunch.

- **Figure out what to fight for.** A crisis heightens our awareness and brings to light what really matters to you, your company, and the services you provide. We learn what we are willing to fight for, whom we trust and who trusts us, and what is valuable to us.

- **A continual crisis mode is abnormal.** Some people seem to feed off a crisis almost like an adrenaline junkie. They may subconsciously create crises and chaos for themselves and those around them. People who grow up in chaotic surroundings, such as with an alcoholic parent, believe that crises are the norm. If a member of your team exhibits this behavior he/she might benefit from professional help.

- **Be solution oriented.** When faced with a crisis don't focus on the problem by saying, "Why did this happen? Why did I make this mistake?" Instead, use "how" and "what" statements like "How can we respond to this issue?" and "What can we do to minimize the damage from this situation?"

- **Be better. NO, be the BEST.** A crisis forces us to be an active learner. Mark Twain said, "The person who grabs the cat by the tail learns 44% faster than the one just watching." New Orleans was forced to learn from Hurricane Katrina. Use a crisis to learn what works and doesn't work within your organization so that your organization can rise to the top.

The Reward of Resiliency

History reminds us that many notable men and women have encountered periods of tough times. Michael Jordan didn't even make his high school basketball team in 10th grade. Jeff Taylor was told that his idea would never work because of its silly name, "monster." We know it now as Monster.com. Albert Einstein struggled in his high school math class. Colonel Sanders' secret recipe was rejected 1,000 times.

People in the Smart Zone are resilient. Resiliency is the ability to bounce back, to get up after you're knocked down, and to improve yourself after a tragic incident. You can keep rewarding yourself with a sense of renewal and resiliency in your personal and professional life using these Smart Ideas:

- **Reframing.** This is the process of shifting from the cup half empty to the cup half full. Some call it serendipity. We have all had bad experiences in our lives. When something goes wrong, look carefully at it, learn from the experience and do things differently the next time.

- **Make work a calling.** In his book, *The 100 Simple Secrets of Happy People,* David Niven, Ph.D. says "If you see your work as only a job, then it's dragging you away from what you really want to be doing. If you see it as a calling, then it is no longer a toiling sacrifice. Instead, it becomes an expression, a part of you." What can you do to find meaning in your work? How can it become an expression of who you are?

- **Be only a little organized.** A survey in *Inc. Magazine* showed that people who claim to have "very neat" desks reported spending 36% more time looking for things than people claiming to have "fairly messy" desks. This implies that there is a productivity cost to neatness. While it isn't realistic for everything in your life to be completely organized, it is imperative that you develop structured approaches to manage the unknown. Be focused on your life goals to head off potential barriers.

- **"Expect things to work out well,"** says resiliency expert Al Siebert, Ph.D. Worrying about failing increases the likelihood of failure. For example, a salesman who is so concerned about his falling sales that he can't bring himself to pick up the phone guarantees that his sales will fall even further. When optimists interpret events 8 out of 10 times they see the positive aspects.

- **Express the right emotions openly.** The shift in our culture to become more compassionate can be tricky in the work environment. This emotional sensitivity in the workplace impacts the bottom line since it affects how we deal with customers, suppliers, clients, and co-workers. Take these steps in expressing emotions: communicate openly and minimize secrets, make decisions that promote the "greater good" versus strict rule compliance, and use humility and empathy when implementing changes.

It's All in How You Think and Respond

As you think about the current crises you are facing, you may only have small crises that you could dismiss and overlook. If the fire isn't threatening your home, then you may dismiss a small flame. Many crises are the result of dismissing a small flame.

It is not about how many crises you experience. It is all about how you think about your crises and how you choose to respond. Those people who are in their Smart Zone—who seem to be the best adjusted and the most resilient—have the best tools in the way they react and the way they think. If you let a crisis define you, then it will be in control of you and affect almost everything you have in your life. If you manage the crisis and don't let it define you, then you don't miss the opportunity to grow because of it. A crisis is a terrible thing to waste. By recognizing a crisis as an opportunity, you are *Working in the Smart Zone.*

PART THREE

*The Ultimate
Smart Moves*

Chapter 24

Top 25 Smart Lifetime Goals

It is extremely important that you not lose sight of the goals that you set for yourself. We aren't just talking about short-term and long-term goals. We are talking about Smart Lifetime Goals. These are the goals that stand the test of time. Smart Lifetime Goals are those you set for yourself that keep you focused on what is important, what you want, and what keeps you productive emotionally, behaviorally, and intellectually—what keeps you in the Smart Zone.

I have taken the liberty of setting 25 Smart Lifetime Goals for you. I also want you to write your own set of Smart Lifetime Goals. Steal no more than 10 of the goals I have written for you here on your own list. Keep your private list individualized, review it every six months, carry it around with you and refer to it when you are making decisions about your business life, your personal life and your overall success. Be loyal to them as much as possible. The 25 Smart Lifetime Goals that follow reflect the teachings of the Smart Zone Model and the Smart Ideas presented already in Part One and Part Two of this book.

My Goals for You

Here are 25 Smart Lifetime Goals, in no deliberate order, that I have set for you:

1. **Be loyal to yourself in the presence of others.** Don't get caught up in being what others want you to be, doing what others want you to do, or saying what others want to hear. Be loyal to yourself when you are alone and when you are with others.

2. **Work to maintain a level of satisfaction, despite your differences.** When we are communicating with other people, we make the mistake of making the issue the most important thing. Instead, the most important thing is to monitor if you are trying to be right at the expense of the relationship. Do you sacrifice the relationship in order to be right?

3. **Watch TV very little and be deliberate when you do.** I'm not against television altogether. I'll take a good episode of a reality TV show anytime. When TV wastes your time, influences your mood, and interferes with your interaction with other people or your other goals, TV is part of the problem.

You can catch updates on most major news stories by going online and spending less than 15 minutes.

4. **Don't abuse the opportunity to get online.** Okay, so the internet is a valuable resource. When you are unaware of how much time you are actually spending online and you use it for recreation when you have other tasks waiting for your attention, you are abusing the opportunity to be online.

5. **Increase your Emotional Intelligence.** Read about EQ, learn about EQ, and improve your EQ by working to decrease the gaps in your ability to manage your emotions and manage yourself.

6. **Use the Smart Zone Life Plan.** We get distracted when we leave our wisdom, our goals, our actions, and our thought processes up to chance. Be deliberate and benefit from the value of the Smart Zone Life Plan provided for you.

7. **Read in your chosen field and read for recreation.** Reading is obviously a way to educate yourself. More important, reading makes you a more interesting person. Many a business relationship is built on common ground and common knowledge. People value learning from others and reading can increase your value and help you work to the best of your ability.

8. **Strive to continually get better.** When you think you know it all, you are ready to die and others are ready to kill you. There is nothing more offensive than being around someone who thinks he or she is the best at something. We can all improve, and so we should all be open to learning. If your company won't pay for training off site, take a day of vacation and pay for the training yourself. You are your best investment.

9. **Be authentic.** Admit when you are wrong, initiate conversation that will be disruptive, be the same in private and in public, and stay engaged in your business and personal relationships.

10. **Eliminate rather than delegate.** To be productive, we think we have to get organized and delegate. The truth is, we should

first seek to eliminate. If you have magazines from two years ago in a pile next to your bed, eliminate them. The information is old and more current issues will use your attention and energy more productively. Do you have 50 pens in your desk drawer yet only use the designer pen you got for your birthday? Eliminate the pens by handing them over to someone else in your company or in your community.

11. **Listen to the feedback others give to you.** Failure is feedback. Others see your blind spots. We grow through pain.

12. **Have accountability partners.** We all benefit from having people in our lives that hold us accountable. When you find someone you'd like to have as an accountability partner—and you can have more than one partner for more than one area of your life—give this person permission to follow up with you, and hold you accountable for specific goals without running the risk of pissing you off. Your partner cannot accept any of your excuses. He or she will keep you solution oriented.

13. **Take inventory of the people that you have in your life.** Work to eliminate toxicity and embellish those who make you better. In a business situation, choose wisely whom you befriend. If morale is low at work, seek to surround yourself with people who are moving forward with healthy attitudes. Be deliberate about networking with people excited about your profession and who model what you value and want to be like.

14. **Take care of your body and your mind.** Exercise, eat right, and live in an environment of optimism and happiness. Studies show that your mental fitness is just as, if not more, important than your physical fitness. Work on the whole package. You are going to have this body for a long time and later you will be glad that you treated it right.

15. **Strive to disrupt yourself every day.** Disrupting yourself doesn't have to hurt—but it should make you uncomfortable. For example, I use a keyboard mouse on my laptop because it's not as easy as using a standard mouse, requires patience, and

it's good to be reminded that I can be disrupted, be resistant, and benefit in the long run. Don't be "disruptive-averse."

16. **Re-evaluate technology.** Too many people think they have to have the latest gadget to be productive. If a BlackBerry doesn't work for you, don't use one. When the iPhone came out, did you think you had to have one? Some technology can only complicate your life. Don't make fun of people still using a Franklin Planner. It works for them. At home, we have, at times, eliminated voicemail on our home phone number. I'm sure you too have multiple phone numbers, email addresses, a fax number, etc. Continually ask yourself if you need to have so many ways to reach you and organize yourself. Re-evaluate and eliminate when possible.

17. **Manage your attention and your energy.** It is not about time management—it's about managing your attention and your energy. Think in terms of your energy and attention being your inventory. Use it wisely and manage it well. No one else is deciding how you can best use this valuable resource.

18. **Don't use your cell phone while you are driving.** You will surely die.

19. **Don't use your cell phone in public where people can hear all about your life.** You will piss people off.

20. **Don't use your cell phone when you are expected to put your attention and energy elsewhere.** You will be telling people they are not important.

21. **Be honest.** You want people to trust you even with bad news.

22. **Have a hobby and invest in your family relationships.** When you retire you need something to look forward to and someone to spend time with. Work to build your identity beyond work.

23. **Pay it forward.** Someone helped you in your career by giving you their attention, introducing you to business contacts, and being your accountability partner. When you are at a point in your career that you can devote the attention and energy, do

the same for someone coming up the ranks who reminds you of yourself. Mentor others.

24. **Don't eat the yellow snow.** Okay, you've heard that one. Have a sense of humor. Be willing to laugh at yourself and your shortcomings—others surely will.

25. **Don't step on Superman's cape.** When others have high aspirations, encourage them to go for it. The only way dreams and goals are achieved is for someone to have them. You can still be the voice of reality and encourage others to achieve success.

Now it is your turn. Write out the 25 Smart Lifetime Goals for yourself, taking no more than 10 from the list I have provided. Think up and document at least 15 or more that are uniquely yours.

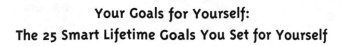

Your Goals for Yourself:
The 25 Smart Lifetime Goals You Set for Yourself

1.

2.

3.

4.

5.

6.

7.

8.

9.

10.

11.

12.

13.

14.

15.

16.

17.

18.

19.

20.

21.

22.

23.

24.

25.

Chapter 25

Catalogue of
Accomplishments

It often happens that we focus on all the things we haven't accomplished. Those are usually easier to list because we are focused on making them happen and may be acutely aware of how close or far they are for us. As you work to be in the Smart Zone, it is important to catalogue your accomplishments both personally and professionally.

Here are some examples of possible personal and professional accomplishments.

Catalogue of Personal Accomplishments:

Example:

1. Set the record for the most goals in a game for my high school soccer team.

2. Learned CPR before finishing college.

3. Attended every home game of the Texas Rangers since 1999.

4. Can still do a cartwheel without hurting myself.

5. Finished my undergraduate degree in 4 years.

6. Paid back my student loans within 2 years of graduating from college.

7. Earned "Volunteer of the Year" for my community involvement.

8. Paid off all our debt except for our house payment and have kept it paid off for more than two years.

9. Attend all my son's soccer games on the weekends.

Catalogue of Professional Accomplishments:

Example:

1. Passed the state bar exam the first try.

2. I am the only associate who has lasted through four CEOs.

3. Have earned pay increases above 5% with every annual review.

4. Have been promoted 4 times in the last 10 years.

5. Persuaded our biggest client to bring all his business to us when other people failed to do so.

6. Saved our company $1.2 million by showing how we could outsource.

In the space provided on the next two pages, begin to catalogue your personal and professional accomplishments. Continue to document them as they happen in the years to come.

Catalogue of Personal Accomplishments:

1.

2.

3.

4.

5.

6.

7.

8.

9.

10.

11.

12.

13.

14.

15.

16.

17.

18.

19.

20.

21.

22.

23.

24.

25.

---　✳　---

Catalogue of Professional Accomplishments:

1.
2.
3.
4.
5.
6.
7.
8.
9.
10.
11.
12.
13.
14.
15.
16.
17.
18.
19.
20.
21.
22.
23.
24.
25.

Chapter 26

The Smart Zone Inventory

Organizations in the Smart Zone

Rate your organization on the following by circling the appropriate response:

Our organization's current level of Emotional Intelligence:

       Terrible   Bad   Okay   Improving   Terrific

Our organization's ability to provide an environment of High Trust:

       Terrible   Bad   Okay   Improving   Terrific

Our organization's ability to Manage Perceptions:

       Terrible   Bad   Okay   Improving   Terrific

Our organization's ability to Communicate Effectively:

       Terrible   Bad   Okay   Improving   Terrific

Our organization's ability to be Solution Oriented:

       Terrible   Bad   Okay   Improving   Terrific

Our organization's ability to provide an environment to Manage Stress:

       Terrible   Bad   Okay   Improving   Terrific

Our organization's ability to manage the presence of Mental Theater:

       Terrible   Bad   Okay   Improving   Terrific

Our organization's ability to Manage Change:

       Terrible   Bad   Okay   Improving   Terrific

Our organization's ability to Manage Mood by providing an optimistic/happy environment:

       Terrible   Bad   Okay   Improving   Terrific

Our organization's support for Sustaining Sanity when it comes to balancing life and work:

       Terrible   Bad   Okay   Improving   Terrific

Our organization's ability to provide an environment of Likeability:

       Terrible   Bad   Okay   Improving   Terrific

Our organization's ability to promote and support the Smart Zone Secret:

       Terrible   Bad   Okay   Improving   Terrific

For those questions that you answered "okay" or below, write down some Smart Ideas regarding that Smart Zone Strategy. Make the list using action-oriented items that are specific to improving your organization's ability to Work in the Smart Zone.

Examples:

1. _Manage Perception:_ When co-workers leave the office early to go to a child's soccer game or a doctor's appointment, I will support them for taking care of themselves and balancing life tasks, especially when that person is always willing to work extra hours to get the job done. I want to be a part of improving the misperception that the person is leaving early and not doing his/her job.

2. _Smart Zone Secret:_ Instead of having an office gift exchange this year we should choose a local charity that represents our interest in the community and ask each person to donate what they can. During the holiday season, we will go to the agency and tour the facility and present them with our gift. This will go a long way to take the focus off of ourselves and give back to the community.

List of Action Steps to Get in the Smart Zone:

1.

2.

3.

4.

5.

Chapter 27

"What I Know For Sure"
Exercise

When people are out of the Smart Zone, many times they focus on the unknowns instead of on the knowns. This is true for CEOs, key leaders, midlevel managers and entry-level positions. Many people are in the habit of focusing on the "what if's" instead of keeping their eye on the knowns. I call it a habit because we have seen people change this habit in the business environment. The most valued employee is typically the one who is able to adapt to change, an important part of being in the Smart Zone.

We have designed a simple technique with powerful results that can be used anywhere without a computer, without fancy graphs and without having to remember the steps. It is called, "What I Know For Sure."

"What I Know For Sure" Exercise

The next time you catch yourself anxious about the unknowns and going through the "What if's" of a business situation, take out a piece of paper—or use a napkin from McDonald's, if that is all you have. This isn't a list you are going to archive.

Now, go to a private place and just start writing out what you <u>do</u> know. This exercise will help you manage your anxiety by helping you focus on what you know rather than on what you don't know. Over time, if you are persistent about doing this exercise whenever you feel out of control and anxious about unknowns, you will develop new ways of thinking. Eventually you will be able to do this exercise automatically in your head without having to write it down.

"What I Know for Sure" Example

Here is an example of focusing on what you know for sure:

Anxiety-provoking thought:

> I just know I am going to be blamed for the company's loss this quarter. It was my project that had trouble getting off the ground. There goes my pay increase, my bonus, and maybe even my title.

What I Know For Sure:

- ✓ My project is new and the projections this quarter were to break even. We did that.
- ✓ My current supervisor told me just yesterday that I would be disappointed in the current quarterly report.
- ✓ The company has said that the fourth quarter reports would be more telling about the success of this project. We just finished the first quarter.

Choose something right now that is creating anxiety and keeping you out of your Smart Zone. Take out a piece of paper. Don't record it in this book. Write at the top of the paper, "What I Know for Sure" and just start writing. As you write, focus on putting things down that are "knowns" rather than "unknowns" and just keep writing. Spelling, grammar, and legibility are not required. This exercise will help you develop GPS thinking and keep your head on straight so that you can continue *Working in the Smart Zone.*

Chapter 28

*Letter to Smart Zone
Significants*

Most of us have a tendency to miss the opportunity to acknowledge what we have gained from other people. All of us have people in our lives that have been:

- accountability partners
- mentors
- influential to us
- teachers
- promoters
- cheerleaders

We all have the tendency to communicate more when something is wrong rather than when everything is fine. That is why, when *Working in the Smart Zone,* it is important to acknowledge those that have made a significant contribution to our personal and business development. I call these people our "Smart Zone Significants."

Choose three people who have been Smart Zone Significants to you in the last three years. Write their names down somewhere on your list of things to do or in your BlackBerry. In the next 10 days, write a letter to each of these people and let them know how important they have been to you and why. Be sure to let them know the result of their significance. That is their reward.

A letter to a Smart Zone Significant should not be in the form of an email, an attachment to an email, or by voicemail. It should be hand-written on a note card, on personal stationary, or on your company stationary. This letter is something each of these people is likely to keep. Hand writing it gives it a very personal touch. It shows that you took the time to think it through and write it by hand, which gives it more value.

Most people let these opportunities pass them by. People who Work in the Smart Zone take the time to acknowledge those who have served the role of a Smart Zone Significant.

Chapter 29

Clinical Issues in the
Workplace

Most business owners and corporate decision makers know that a mentally healthy workforce is linked to:

- Lower total medical costs
- Lower absenteeism
- Increased productivity
- Decreased disability costs
- A more satisfying workplace

According to The Partnership for Workplace Health:

- It is estimated that perhaps 25% of people of working age deal with mental illness and/or substance abuse in any given year
- Mental illness and substance abuse annually cost employers an estimated $80 billion to $100 billion in indirect costs
- More workers are absent from work because of stress and anxiety than because of physical illness or injury
- Stress and depression probably explain close to 30% of the total risk of heart attacks
- Mental illness short-term disability claims are growing by 10% annually and can account for 30% or more of the corporate disability claims for the typical employer
- According to the Surgeon General, 1 in 5 adults will experience a diagnosable mental illness in any given year. About 15% of those will also experience a co-occurring substance abuse disorder.

Despite these statistics, less than one-third of adults with a diagnosable mental disorder receive treatment in any given year.

Depression

Everyone feels "down in the dumps" or "blue" sometimes. Feeling sad is a normal part of life. But when sadness interferes with everyday functioning, it is a more serious condition.

Depression impacts normal life functioning at work and at home. It is estimated that 9.5% of the population, 20.9 million American adults, suffer from depressive illness. People are often afraid to admit that they

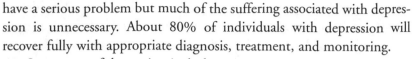

have a serious problem but much of the suffering associated with depression is unnecessary. About 80% of individuals with depression will recover fully with appropriate diagnosis, treatment, and monitoring.

Symptoms of depression include:

- Persistent sad, anxious, or "empty" mood
- Feelings of hopelessness, pessimism
- Feelings of guilt, worthlessness, helplessness
- Loss of interest or pleasure in hobbies and activities that were once enjoyed, including sex
- Decreased energy, fatigue, being "slowed down"
- Difficulty concentrating, remembering, making decisions
- Insomnia, early-morning awakening, or oversleeping
- Appetite and/or weight loss or overeating and weight gain
- Thoughts of death or suicide; suicide attempts
- Restlessness, irritability
- Persistent physical symptoms that do not respond to treatment, such as headaches, digestive disorders, and chronic pain

If any of these behaviors are occurring in your life, then you may be suffering from the effects of depression.

The good news is that the symptoms of depression are treatable and can be managed through expert therapy and medications. The problem with treatment may surprise you. The real problem is that people don't seek treatment, not that the treatments are ineffective. The stigma associated with depression hinders many people from asking questions during routine physical exams or being honest when asked questions about their symptoms.

Undiagnosed depression can be life altering and life threatening. It's important to find a therapist who is able to treat depression and help a person get out of the "fog" that depression creates.

Depression impacts mind, body and spirit. It affects eating, sleeping and feelings of self-worth. Remember, depression is not a sign of weakness or a condition that can be willed or wished away. People with depression cannot simply "snap out of it" and get better. A depressed person needs support, gentle guidance and someone to listen. Friends and family can help a depressed person by helping him or her to get treatment and find a therapist who will work in collaboration with a physician who can evaluate for medication.

Depression and its effects on an individual's well-being is clearly understood. However, it's key to create a partnership with a knowledgeable therapist who has experience treating depression.

Anxiety

Anxiety is about the future. Remember, *worry is the misuse of imagination*. Someone who has feelings of fear is someone who has trouble staying in the present. We see a lot of adults with anticipatory anxiety in our clinical practice and in working with key leaders onsite in organizations.

> James D., 46, is a midlevel manager who has been with the same automobile company since he was 17 years old. Over the years he has been promoted several times, and now oversees a team of 12 sales people.
>
> Behind his back his direct reports call him "Nervous Nellie" and make fun of his motivational style. James has been to a lot of sales and management trainings. He knows that his attitude is important. He also knows that he sets the mood for the rest of his department. Because James lives by the mantra, "You are only as good as your next sale," he is always nervous about the numbers each quarter. That makes it difficult for him to motivate himself, his co-workers and his direct reports.
>
> James suffers from anticipatory anxiety, meaning that he gets nervous and fearful *before* an event happens. He remembers always being nervous before a test in school, sweating profusely before dates in college, and talking himself out of taking risks throughout his life. He realizes he has stayed with his current employer because it would be too risky to go and work for someone else with so many unknowns.

James was identified as a key leader in an organization we consulted with that was getting ready to have new owners. James was unaware that the current owners were looking to sell the business. We were brought in to provide Smart Zone Training to help key employees promote more productivity among their direct reports. The ROI was to increase employee engagement, improve internal communication, build a High Trust environment, and promote an increase in emotional intelligence-all involving Smart Zone strategies.

Working with James one on one, I had the opportunity to assess his emotional intelligence using the EQ-i (listed in the Glossary of this book). That information helped me show him how to get quick relief from anxiety. James disclosed that he had been in therapy in the past and that the therapy seemed to make his anxiety worse.

Studies show that traditional talk therapy, in which someone reviews their past and tells stories about events that have been full of anxiety, actually creates more anxiety. Instead, cognitive behavioral therapy (CBT) is a better option. This is manageable in an organizational setting when we consult onsite with key leaders. CBT focuses on retraining your brain to think differently and modifying your behavior in the past. That is exactly what we do when we teach people about Mental Theater in the Smart Zone model (see Chapter 8). It has been reported that 47% of patients with Generalized Anxiety Disorder report improvement six months after learning to use CBT strategies, compared with 17% of those who receive traditional analytical psychotherapy.

One of the tasks that I gave to James was the "What I Know For Sure" Exercise (Chapter 27). By doing this task five times a day for two weeks, James was able to stay in the present and manage his anxiety. This approach works because it trains your thought process to go in a different direction helping you focus on what you know for sure rather than on the unknowns. Unknowns are like lighter fluid on anxiety. Moving your thoughts in a different direction keeps the anxiety at a manageable level. James knew it wouldn't be easy, but he was willing to try.

More than 13% of the adult U.S. population suffers from an anxiety disorder. People with anxiety disorders see a doctor three to five times more often than those without anxiety disorders.

Bipolar Disorder

Bipolar Disorder is a very misunderstood disorder. Formerly referred to as Manic Depression, Bipolar Disorder is a serious condition that causes shifts in a person's mood, energy, and ability to function on a daily basis. When a person has Bipolar Disorder, their mood swings are much more severe than the normal ups and downs that most people experience.

Symptoms of Bipolar Disorder include:

- Increased energy, activity, and restlessness
- Excessively "high," overly good, euphoric mood
- Extreme irritability
- Racing thoughts and talking very fast, jumping from one idea to another
- Distractibility, inability to concentrate
- Little need for sleep
- Unrealistic beliefs in one's abilities and powers
- Poor judgment
- Risk-taking behaviors
- Increased sex drive
- Episodic spending sprees
- Abuse of drugs
- Provocative, intrusive, or aggressive behavior
- Denial

There is concern among the professional community that Bipolar Disorder tends to be over diagnosed. It is important that a psychologist, psychiatrist or medical professional trained in the diagnosis of Bipolar Disorder carefully monitor a person and obtain accurate information about history and clinical presentation before making the diagnosis.

While Bipolar Disorder is a serious diagnosis, more information is now available regarding the use of medications and therapy to treat the symptoms once properly diagnosed. It is also important to have family support to help a person with Bipolar Disorder learn to cope. In a work environment it is important for a person's mood to be stabilized so they are better able to concentrate and tend to their job responsibilities. Left untreated, many (but not all) people with Bipolar Disorder have difficulty keeping jobs and getting along with other people.

Attention-Deficit/Hyperactivity Disorder (AD/HD)

Attention-Deficit/Hyperactivity Disorder (AD/HD) is not just for kids. It is estimated that two-thirds of children will still meet the criteria for the disorder as adults. Without the development of compensatory strategies, AD/HD can cause difficulty at work, in relationships, and in normal daily functioning.

The three main symptoms assessed for AD/HD are inattentiveness, impulsivity, and hyperactivity. There is also another subset of symptoms being investigated called "Sluggish Cognitive Tempo." While AD/HD is not a learning disability, it does tend to interfere with a person's ability to learn. In a work environment, this can manifest as:

- Needing to hear directions more than once
- Difficulty staying organized
- Inability to manage everyday tasks
- Needing to receive constant reminders
- Projects left incomplete
- Tardiness
- Poor memory
- Difficulty managing impulses
- Difficulty sitting still and managing distractions

The term AD/HD was previously used solely for the hyperactive form of the disorder, while the term ADD (Attention-Deficit Disorder) was reserved for the form without hyperactivity. However, in the past few years, the term AD/HD has become the primary term for all forms of this disorder. To further describe the disruptive symptoms, AD/HD has three subtypes:

- Primarily Inattentive
- Primarily Impulsive-Hyperactive
- Combined Type (indicating all three symptoms are present)

It is believed that AD/HD is a disorder of the frontal lobe. The symptoms do not suddenly occur with a new job or with difficulty getting along with your cube mate. The symptoms typically appear before the age of seven and are present in more than one setting. For an adult, the two settings are at home and at work. Typically a person with AD/HD will do better in a setting that is more structured, where there are opportunities for redirection, where there is constant accountability, and there are systems in place to stay organized.

Substance Abuse

More than 8% of full-time workers (12.7 million people) have drinking problems. Twenty percent of workers say that they have been injured, have had to cover for a co-worker, or needed to work harder because of another employee's drinking, which leads to decreased productivity, increased indirect costs, and a host of other workplace problems (George Washington Medical Center, 2002). A study by the Substance Abuse and Mental Health Services Administration estimated that there are 16.4 million current illicit drug users with full-time jobs, who are posing significant risks to their own health and productivity and to others around them.

Signs of possible substance abuse include:

- Chronic absenteeism
- Frequent tardiness
- Extended "breaks" at work
- Decrease in usual productivity
- Smell of alcohol on his/her breath
- Impaired motor skills
- Noticeable changes in personality
- Less efficiency than normal

- More irritability
- Poor emotional control
- Persistent forgetfulness
- Dulled mental abilities
- Frequent mood swings
- Unusual number of physical complaints
- Poor concentration
- Inappropriate behavior for the workplace
- Numerous discussions of substance-related behaviors/topics

Substance abuse is a treatable disorder. Between 40% and 60% of patients treated appropriately for alcoholism and/or other drug use disorders remain abstinent after a year; another 15% resume drinking, though not to the point where they become dependent again. This is comparable to the effectiveness of treatments for other chronic diseases such as diabetes, high blood pressure, and asthma (George Washington Medical Center, 2002).

The information provided is not a complete listing of symptoms and treatment for any of these disorders. Please consult a medical professional for more information about these disorders and for proper diagnosis and treatment.

For detailed information regarding clinical issues for children, refer to my other book, *Parenting in the Smart Zone*, available through our website www.SmartZoneExpert.com.

Chapter 30

Final Words for
Working in the Smart Zone

Over the years in our clinical practice and in our consulting business, we have worked with thousands of people who have reported a disturbing trend. We hear story after story of people making mistakes that they wouldn't ordinarily make. These mistakes range from the smaller mistakes of forgetting something at work to overlooking critical details that could mean lost profit, lost productivity, and lost peace of mind. Now that you are familiar with the Smart Zone Model, you know that the trend we noticed was what we now call being out of the Smart Zone.

We know that companies benefit when employees and key leaders are *Working in the Smart Zone.* Using the two fundamental concepts of Emotional Intelligence and Trust and the 10 strategies outlined in the Smart Zone Model, every organization can benefit from learning about the Smart Zone and practicing the strategies. By incorporating the concepts of the Smart Zone Life Plan you can move in the direction of Intentional Success.

Everyone can benefit from using the Smart Zone strategies at home and at work to increase productivity. Being in the Smart Zone is the key to outperforming, outlasting, creating satisfaction, and beating the competition.

Now that you know the Smart Zone Model, have what you need to develop a Smart Zone Life Plan, and have learned the Ultimate Smart Moves, you are ready to put it all into action. To be the most effective, tell people what you are doing to Work in the Smart Zone to create a climate of accountability. Ask people to join you in the Smart Zone and introduce Smart Zone ideas to others who would also benefit from what you have learned. Share this book with others and build a Smart Zone community.

Tell us your stories by emailing me at Susan@SmartZoneExpert.com. If you haven't signed up for our electronic newsletter, do so right now on the home page of www.SmartZoneExpert.com. Every month we will bring you the latest in Smart Zone strategies that you can use to increase your productivity and manage your energy and attention. Forward our newsletter to a friend and present the ideas to your coworkers. If you have a Smart Zone idea of your own, we would love to hear it. We want to know how *Working in the Smart Zone* works for you and your organ-

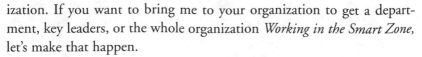

ization. If you want to bring me to your organization to get a department, key leaders, or the whole organization *Working in the Smart Zone,* let's make that happen.

By using one Smart Zone Strategy at a time, you will increase productivity—first with yourself, then with your organization, and possibly with your community. You can do your part to create a new trend and get yourself and others moving in the right direction—*Working in the Smart Zone.*

Glossary

Accountability Mechanisms: People or systems a person puts in place to catch him or her when he or she deviates from his or her Smart Zone Life Plan. Developing Accountability Mechanisms is a way to build self-trust and to use the trust a person has in others to hold him or her to the goal.

Adaptability: The ability to manage change.

Anxiety: A physiological state characterized by cognitive, emotional, behavioral, and somatic components that combine to create feelings often labeled as fear, apprehension, or worry.

Attention-Deficit/Hyperactivity Disorder: Also known as AD/HD, is a development disorder that impairs one's ability to keep focused

Baby Boomer: This generation has been called the "Me Generation" and enjoys being involved, valued and needed. Boomers are optimistic and strive to find fulfillment at work. They are willing to work all hours, often taking it to the workaholic level. Typically born between 1946 and 1960.

Bar-On EQ-i: The BarOn Emotional Quotient Inventory (EQ-i) is an online assessment that can be done on an individual basis. Based on more than 20 years of research worldwide, the BarOn EQ-i examines an individual's emotional and social strengths and weaknesses. The Framework for Emotional Competencies is as follows:

BarOn EQ-i® Model

Intrapersonal	Emotional Self-Awareness Assertiveness Independence Self-Regard Self-Actualization
Interpersonal	Empathy Social Responsibility Interpersonal Relationships
Stress Management	Stress Tolerance Impulse Control
Adaptability	Problem Solving Reality Testing Flexibility
General Mood	Happiness Optimism

Bipolar Disorder: A condition defined as recurrent episodes of significant disturbance in mood that can occur on a spectrum that ranges from debilitating depression to unbridled mania.

Brand Trust: Trust in a particular brand or product that builds confidence in a consumer.

Bucket Theory of Stress: The theory that everyone has a metaphorical bucket inside of him or her that gets full when there are stressful events. It is important to anticipate the stressful events and empty his or her bucket to make room for the stress and avoid an exaggerated response.

Cognitive Behavioral Therapy (CBT): A type of therapy based on modifying thoughts, assumptions, beliefs and behaviors to influence more accurate and helpful ways of thinking. It is what is addressed in the Mental Theater strategy in the Smart Zone model.

Compassion Fatigue: When there is suffering emotionally from someone else's pain and suffering. Also called "Empathy Distress."

Current Life Mode: The one a person wants to change in the Looking Back part of the Smart Zone Life Plan. It tells about the way a person thinks that keeps him or her out of the Smart Zone.

Depression: A clinical term for a state of intense sadness, melancholia or despair that has advanced to the point of being disruptive to an individual's social functioning and/or activities of daily living

Disruptive-Averse: An out-of-the-Smart-Zone phenomenon when someone avoids the opportunity to be disrupted, be resistant, and benefit in the long run. Being uncomfortable and disrupted promotes growth and is part of being in your Smart Zone.

Emotional Competency: The skill of expressing emotions that are appropriate to the situation and a person's needs and not seeking to suppress emotions in others.

Emotional Intelligence: A set of competencies that distinguish how people manage feelings, interact, and communicate.

Empathy: The ability to recognize, acknowledge, and experience other people's feelings.

Engagement: The process of an employee being totally present and mentally involved in a task, a mission, or a belief within an organization.

Eustress: Good stress.

Exaggerated Response: When a person overreacts to a stressor.

Failure: This equals feedback.

Faulty Thinking: This type of thinking is the type a person wants to change and tends to be problem focused, negative, self-defeating, hopeless, and dead-end in nature.

Flow: The mental state of operation in which the person is fully immersed in what he or she is doing, characterized by a feeling of energized focus, full involvement, and success in the process of the activity. Proposed by psychologist Mihaly Csikszentmihalyi, the concept has been widely referenced across a variety of fields.

Friendliness: The ability to communicate liking and openness to others.

Generation X: Characterized as independent and resourceful, and tending to value a network of close, reliable friends. Some may view them as impatient and willing to throw out tried-and-true strategies. Born between 1961 and 1980.

Generation Y: Also called the Millennials, this techno-savvy generation has never known life without computers and grew up in an atmosphere of diversity and collaboration. Typically born 1981 to the present.

Good Stress: The type of stress that motivates a person to action, getting his or her adrenaline pumping to bring passion and excitement to whatever a person is doing. Sometimes referred to as eustress.

GPS Beliefs: Those beliefs that are continually course corrected. GPS Beliefs work in much the same way as a Global Positioning System. GPS Beliefs, just like the device, get a person to a destination with course correction occurring when he or she gets off track.

GPS Goals: Goals that are the result of GPS Thinking. These goals are the kind that keep a person on track to be in the Smart Zone.

GPS Thinking: The kind of thinking that keeps a person on track and course corrects him or her to be in the Smart Zone. This type of thinking is documented in the Moving Forward portion of the Smart Zone Life Plan.

Happiness: An emotion in which a person experiences feelings ranging from contentment and satisfaction to bliss and intense joy.

Gross National Happiness: A way of defining quality of life in more holistic and psychological terms than the traditional Gross National Product. Bhutan's King Jigme Singye came up with the term in 1972. The king claims the concept is based on the premise that true development of human society takes place when material and spiritual development occur side by side to complement and reinforce each other.

High Trust: When there is greater confidence in a person or organization.

Hybrid Leaders: The blending of the best of the male and female leadership styles. This concept was developed by Trudy Bourgeois.

Integrity: Sticking to your code of conduct. It's basing your actions on an internally consistent framework of principles.

Intentional Success: Planned success. It is the kind to write about in a Smart Zone Life Plan. It is the kind of success that is deliberate and well thought out.

Intuition: Understanding without apparent effort, quick and ready insight seemingly independent of previous experiences or empirical knowledge.

Leadership: A person who can instill passion and direction to an individual or group of individuals.

Likeability: The ability to create positive attitudes in other people through the delivery of functional and psychological benefits (According to Tim Sanders).

Mental Theater: The creation of a "drama" in a person's head so it seems as if the event actually happened.

Millennials: Also called Generation Y, this techno-savvy generation has never known life without computers and grew up in an atmosphere of diversity and collaboration. Typically born 1981 to the present.

Non-Negotiable Necessities: Those things that a person values and believes that when you honor them, you build self-trust.

Old/Negative/Irrational Beliefs: Those beliefs that keep a person out of the Smart Zone. They are the beliefs that keep a person looking back rather than moving forward in his or her thinking.

Operational Agility: The ability of an organization or individual to sense and respond to operation or business opportunities in order to stay innovative and competitive in a turbulent and quickly changing business environment.

Optimism: An outlook on life such that one maintains a view of the world as a positive place. It is the opposite of pessimism. Optimists generally believe that people and events are inherently good, so that most situations work out in the end for the best.

Pay-it-Forward Mentality: Thinking in such a way that a person looks for ways to give back to others the ways others have given to him or her.

People Smart: The common sense that helps people understand other people.

Platform of Trust: It is attainable in any relationship at work and at home and it is important to keep it steady and strong to build confidence in what a person says, does, and feels.

Positive Affirmations: Self statements that are supportive in nature that are said by a person over and over to him or herself. Positive Affirmations are part of having good, healthy mental theater.

Problem Focused: "Why" questions that generate answers that focus on the problem.

Realness: The integrity that stands behind a person's likeability and guarantees it's authenticity.

Reframing: This is the process of shifting from the cup half empty to the cup half full.

Relevance: The ability to connect with the interests, wants, and needs of other people.

Responsible: Means being able to be counted on.

Quit and Stay: When an employee stops being engaged at work, does the bare minimum and continues to take up space in the work environment. The person stays just below the radar so work performance does not suffer too much. Most likely not a team player.

Resiliency: The ability to bounce back, to get up after you're knocked down, and to improve yourself after a tragic incident.

Sandwich Generation: A generation who cares for their parents as well as their own children who still live at home.

Self-Management Skills: Skills that help a person cope better with work pressures.

Self-Trust: Honoring your own non-negotiable necessities and your intuition to build your own internal trust.

Sleep Test: A simple test that helps a person know if he or she is doing the right thing. It is the answer to keeping your sanity sustained and involves asking yourself the question, "Do you make it right with yourself?"

Sluggish Cognitive Tempo: A subset of symptoms that are similar to AD/HD.

Smart Lifetime Goals: These are the goals a person sets for himself or herself that keeps him or her focused on what is important, what he or she wants, and what keeps him or her productive emotionally, behaviorally, and intellectually. These goals keep a person in the Smart Zone.

Self-Soothe: To use internal resource to calm down so a person's anxiety level decreases.

Smart Zone: A mental state where a person works to the best of his or her ability emotionally, intellectually, and behaviorally. People in the Smart Zone are more productive.

Smart Zone Competency: Predetermined traits for a person in the Smart Zone that helps him or her to properly perform a specific aspect of being in the Smart Zone as a lifestyle or as a business person. It encompasses a combination of knowledge, skills, and behavior used to improve productivity and performance.

Smart Zone Life Plan: A set of strategies and worksheets that give the tools to develop the *6 Competencies for a Business Person* and the *8 Competencies for a Smart Zone Lifestyle*.

Smart Zone Model: Consists of two key concepts-Emotional Intelligence and Trust-and the 10 strategies that keep individuals and organizations in the Smart Zone.

Smart Sandwich Model: A structure for communication that brings intentional success. It consists of three parts and helps keep people communicating in the Smart Zone.

Smart Zone Secret: Take the focus off of yourself. By becoming outwardly focused on others we can generate positive energy and create an atmosphere of collaboration and encouragement. Organizations and individuals can practice the Smart Zone Secret.

Smart Zone Significants: People in your life you should acknowledge that have made a significant contribution to your personal and business development.

Smart Zone Thinking: Solution oriented thinking that keeps people in the mindset of working to the best of their ability emotionally, intellectually and behaviorally. This is the kind of thinking used when Moving Forward (outlined in the Smart Zone Life Plan).

Snow White: Disney character that is the poster child for Smart Zone thinking, Emotional Intelligence, and Trust.

Social Competency: The ability to achieve personal goals in social interaction while simultaneously maintaining positive relationships with others over time and across situations.

Solution Oriented: When a person is focused on the solution instead of the problem in the way he or she acts, thinks, and feels. Uses "how" and "what" statements like "How can we respond to this issue?" and "What can we do to minimize the damage from this situation?" Does not tend to use "why" questions which focus on the problem.

Stress Kindling: This happens when you continually add to your stress level, a little bit at a time.

Substance Abuse: The use of any legal or illegal substance that when used causes damage to the person's physical and/or mental health and causes the person legal, social, financial or other problems including endangering their lives or the lives of others. It is not dependent on the amount or the type of substance.

Sympathy: When a person feels compassion for someone, but this is the person's feeling only and does not focus on what others are feeling.

Time Management: A technique used by rookies. Seasoned Smart Zone followers manage attention and energy—not time.

Toxic Influences: Those influences which are able to produce illness or damage to a relationship or a person. It is also used to describe toxic effects on larger and more complex groups, such as the family unit or "society at large."

Traditionalist: Known as the "Silent Generation," traditionalists have a "We will prevail" attitude and are characterized by loyalty, duty and conformity. Some may see them as rigid and dictatorial. Typically born between 1925-45.

Triangles: They are relationship poison. Triangles are formed when two co-workers have a disagreement, and they involve a third, less powerful person to diffuse the conflict rather than resolving the disagreement between themselves. With this process, called "triangulation," the problem can become bigger than it needs to be.

Trust: The lubrication that makes it possible for organizations to work. Trust is a relationship of reliance. A trusted person is presumed to seek to fulfill their previous promises.

Ultimate Smart Moves: These include some of the Smart Moves from Part One that provide such high value that they deserve their own chapters. Smart Moves are strategies that keep you in your Smart Zone.

"What" and "How" Questions: The type of questions that get people talking about the solution.

"Why" Questions: The type of questions that get people talking about the problem.

Wisdom: A trait that can be developed by experience, but not taught. It may be possessed independent of experience or complete knowledge. It is often looked at as his/her ideals and principles that govern all actions and decisions. Applications of personal wisdom include the ethical and social guidelines that determine the nature of short- and long-term goals pursued in life.

Yuck Factor: This is the part of your workday where your productivity plummets. It can also be a task, report or other event that consistently causes you to say, "Yuck!"

About the Author

As a licensed psychologist currently in private practice and a sought after professional speaker, Susan gets right to the point. Her presentations offer a new perspective to help others better manage change and increase productivity in their lives. Her dynamic presentations are uniquely tailored to the needs of each audience after careful collaboration with program planners and meeting professionals.

Susan is available to consult with individuals and organizations in need of expert direction to increase productivity, manage conflict and create a culture of collaboration and engagement. Conflicting values and behavioral styles often interfere with success in the workplace. Susan can provide specialized training to leaders and/or employees that will arm them with the skills to meet today's workplace challenges.

Contact Susan for corporate programs, educational events, and other speaking opportunities by emailing her at Susan@SmartZoneExpert.com. Susan will engineer the experience from beginning to end to develop the most valuable program possible.

About Smart Zone Solutions

For information about products by Susan Fletcher, Ph.D. and her private practice visit: www.FletcherPhD.com

Books:
 Working in the Smart Zone
 Parenting in the Smart Zone

Pocket Guide:
 Working in the Smart Zone

Special Report Audio CD's:
(See www.SmartZoneExpert.com for descriptions)
 Attention-Deficit/Hyperactivity Disorder (AD/HD)
 Childhood Depression
 Learning Disabilities
 Adult Depression

For information about hiring Susan Fletcher, Ph.D. as a speaker or leadership development consultant, please visit: www.SmartZoneExpert.com

For information:
 Susan Fletcher, Ph.D.
 Smart Zone Solutions
 2301 Ohio Drive, Suite 135
 Plano, Texas 75093
 (877) 447.8726

Websites:
 www.SmartZoneExpert.com
 www.FletcherPhD.com

References

Chapter 2 – Emotional Intelligence

Egon Zehnder, www.egonzehnder.com

Hay/McBer Research and Innovation Group (1997). This research was provided to Daniel Goleman and is reported in his book (Goleman, 1998).

McClelland, D. C. (1999). Identifying competencies with behavioral-event interviews. *Psychological Science, 9*(5), 331-339.

Center for Creative Leadership: www.ccl.org

Spencer, L. M., Jr. & Spencer, S. (1993). Competence at work: Models for superior performance. New York: John Wiley and Sons.

Spencer, L. M. J., McClelland, D. C., & Kelner, S. (1997). Competency assessment methods: History and state of the art. Boston: Hay/McBer.

Pesuric, A., & Byham, W. (1996, July). The new look in behavior modeling: Training and development, 25-33.

Porras, J. I., & Anderson, B. (1981). Improving managerial effectiveness through modeling-based training. *Organizational Dynamics, 9*, 60-77.

Boyatzis, R. (1982). The competent manager: A model for effective performance. New York: John Wiley and Sons.

Lusch, R. F., & Serpkeuci, R. (1990). Personal differences, job tension, job outcomes, and store performance: A study of retail managers. *Journal of Marketing.*

Seligman, M. E. P. (1990). Learned optimism. New York: Knopf.

Walter V. Clarke Associates. (1996). Activity vector analysis: Some applications to the concept of emotional intelligence. Pittsburgh, PA: Walter V. Clarke Associates.

Hay/McBer Research and Innovation Group (1997). This research was provided to Daniel Goleman and is reported in his book (Goleman, 1998).

Bachman, J., Stein, S., Campbell, K., & Sitarenios, G. (2000). Emotional intelligence in the collection of debt. *International Journal of Selection and Assessment,* 8(3), 176-182.

Military Recruiting: The Department of Defense Could Improve Its Recruiter Selection and Incentive Systems: GAO report" submitted to Congress January 30, 1998.

Chapter 3 – The Trust Factor

Covey, Stephen M. R. (2006). The speed of trust. Free Press.

Chapter 5 – Communication

Goleman, Daniel (1998). Emotional Intelligence: Why it can matter more than IQ. Bantam.

Chapter 6 – Solution Oriented

Sacks, Danielle. (October, 2006). How open-source design (and a big shot of fashion) saved Puma, and invented an industry. *Fast Company,* (109), 58.

Chapter 7 – Managing Stress

Executive EQ, Cooper, R. K, and Sawaf, A. (1998). Executive EQ. Perigee Trade.

Chapter 9 – Managing Change

Fishman, Charles. (July 1998). The War for Talent. *Fast Company,* (16), 108.

Chapter 10 – Managing Mood

Seligman, M. E. P. (1990). Learned optimism. New York: Knopf.

Collins, J. & Porras, J. I. (2004). Built to last: Successful habits of visionary companies. Collins.

Collins, J. (2001). Good to great: Why some companies make the leap... and others don't. Collins.

Goleman, D. (2007) Social intelligence: The new science of human relationships. Bantam Press.

Chapter 12 – Likeability

Estroff Marano, Hara. (1998). Why doesn't anybody like me? Harper Paperbacks.

Sanders, Tim (2006). The likeability factor: How to boost your L-Factor and achieve your life's dreams. Three Rivers Press.

PsyMax Solutions. This research was provided by "The Herman Trend Alert," by Roger Herman and Joyce Gioia, Strategic Business Futurists. The Herman Trend Alert is a trademark of The Herman Group, Inc." www.hermangroup.com.

Chapter 18 – Smart Zone Thinking

Galinsky, A. D., Magee, J. C., Inesi, M. E., & Gruenfeld, D. H. (2006). Power and perspectives not taken. *Psychological Science,* 17, 1068-1074.

Chapter 20 – Getting in the Flow

Staff (February, 2007). I no longer want to work for money, *Fast Company.* (112), 112.

Tice, Carol (February, 2007). Building the 21st century leader. *Entrepreneur Magazine,* February 2007, (35, No. 2), 64.

Bourgeois, Trudy (2005). The hybrid leader: Blending the best of the male and female leadership styles. Oakhill Press.

Chapter 22 – Generation Smart Zone

Heffernan, Margaret (January, 2006). Managing generational differences in the workplace. *Fast Company Resource Center online.*

Chapter 23 – A Crisis is a Terrible Thing to Waste

Niven, David. (2006). The 100 simple secrets of happy people: What scientists have learned and how you can use it. HarperOne.

Freedman, David (December, 2006). Go ahead, make a mess. *Inc. Magazine,* (28, No. 12), 120.

Chapter 29 – Clinical Issues in the Workplace

Partnership for Workplace Health, A program of the American Psychiatric Foundation. www.workplacementalhealth.org.

Statistic for Depression, Anxiety, Biplolar Disorder, and Substance abuse provided by the National Institute of Mental Health (NIMH).

Ensuring Solutions to Alcohol Problems, George Washington Medical Center, December, 2002.

Substance Abuse and Mental Health Services Administration, United States Department of Health and Human Services.